MUSLIMS IN MEGHALAYA

Muhammad Hasibor Rahman

KITAB BHAVAN
NEW DELHI-1100 02 (INDIA)

Kitab Bhavan
1790, Kalan Mahal, Daryaganj,
New Delhi – 110002
Phone: 011-23277392/93, 23274686;
Fax: 91-11-23263383
Email: nasri@vsnl.com

First Edition 2004

ISBN: 81-7151-353-0

Laser Typesetting at:
Laser Track
Kalan Mahal, Darya Ganj,
New Delhi-1100 02 (India)

Published by
Nusrat Ali Nasri for Kitab Bhavan
1784, Kalan Mahal, Daryaganj
New Delhi – 110002

Printed in India at:
Nice Printing Press
Khureji Khas, Delhi-110051

Contents

List of Plates

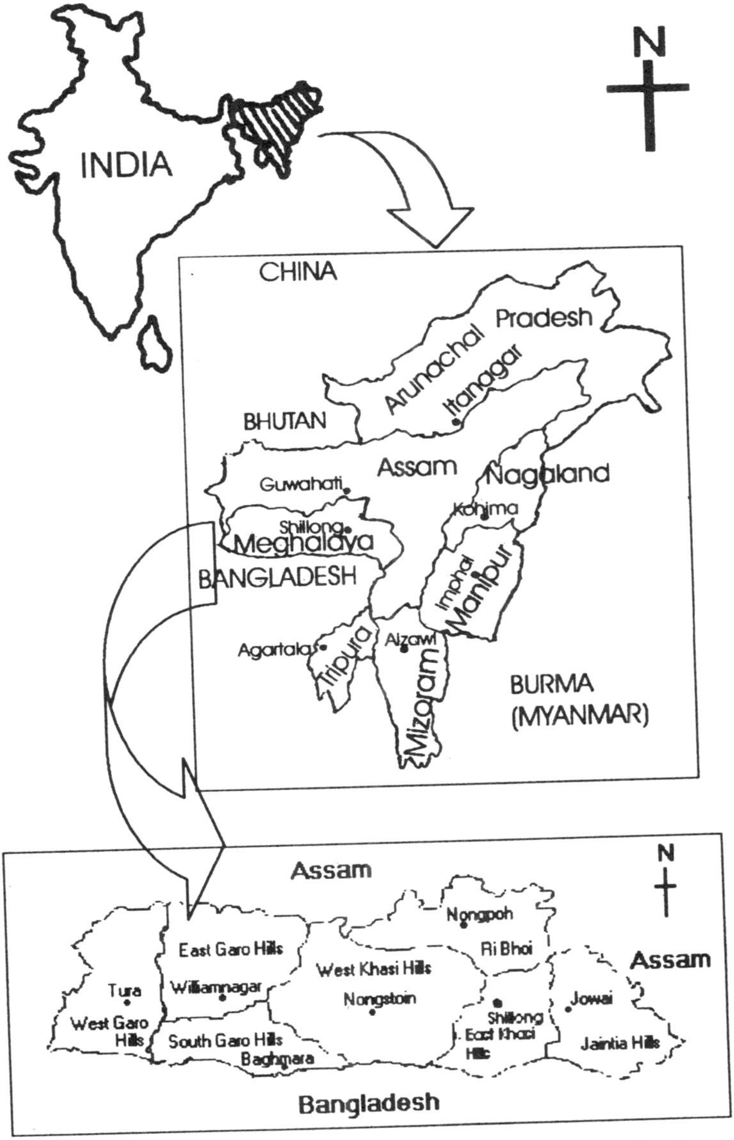

Plate 1: Location of Meghalaya in North East India
(Maps not to scale)

Plate 2: Mosque at Laban, Shillong

Plate 3: Mosque at Laitumkhrah, Shillong

Plate 4: Tomb of Mir Jumlah

Plate 5: Tomb of Sayed Sulaiman Chisti

Plate 6: Tomb of Shah Safreen Shah

Plate 7: Tomb of Shah Nur Muhammad Shah

Plate 8: Muslim graveyard at Mawprem

Plate 9: Muslim graveyard at Laban

Plate 10: Dawki suspension bridge

Plate 11: Dawki Mosque

Plate 12: Mosque at William Nagar Bazar

Plate 13: Residence of Sir Syeed Muhammad Saadullah at Risa Colony, Shillong

Plate 14: Mosque at New Bhaitbari, West Garo Hills

Plate 15: Darul Ulum Madrasah at New Bhaitbari, West Garo Hills

List of Tables

Message of the Holy Qur'an

[1]

O mankind! Be careful of your duty to your Lord who created you from a single soul and from it created his mate and from them twain hath spread abroad a multitude of men and women. Be careful of your duty toward Allah in Whom ye claim [your rights] of one another, and toward the wombs [that bore you]. Lo! Allah hath been a Watcher over you. [IV: I]

[2]

And we have given you [mankind] power in the earth and appointed for you therein livelihood. [VII: 10]

[3]

And when the prayer is ended, then disperse in the land and seek Allah's bounty and remember Allah much, that ye may be successful. [LXII: 10]

[4]

O mankind! Eat of that which is lawful and wholesome in the earth; and follow not the footsteps of the devil. Lo! He is an open enemy for you. [II: 168]

[5]

Lo! Allah changeth not the condition of a folk until they [first] ge that which is in their hearts. [XII; 11]

[6]

Unto the men [of a family] belongeth a share of that which parents and near kindred leave, and unto the women a share of that which parents and near kindred leave, whether it be little or much—a legal share. [IV: 7]

[7]

Lo! Allah commandeth you that ye restore deposits to their owners, and if you judge between mankind, that ye judge justly. [IV: 58]

[8]

O ye who believe! Squander not your wealth among yourselves in vanity, except it be a trade by mutual consent, and kill not one another. Lo! Allah is ever Merciful unto you. [IV: 29]

[9]

And strive for Allah with the endeavour which is His right. He hath chosen you and hath not laid upon you in religion any hardship; the faith of your father Abraham [is yours]. He hath named you Muslims of old time and in this [Scripture], that the messenger may be a witness against you, and that ye may be witnesses against mankind. So establish worship, pay the poor due and hold fast to Allah. He is your protecting Friend. A blessed Patron and a blessed Helper. [XXII: 78]

[10]

Those who spend [of that which Allah hath given them] in ease and adversity, those who control their wrath and are forgiving toward mankind; Allah loveth the good. [III: 134]

[11]

Unto each nation have we given sacred rights which they are to perform; so let them not dispute with thee of the matter. [XXII: 67]

[12]

There is no compulsion in religion. The right direction is henceforth distinct from error. [II: 256]

[13]

Allah hath blighted usury and made alms giving fruitful. Allah loveth not the impious and guilty. [II: 276]

[14]

A kind word with forgiveness is better than alms giving followed by injury. Allah is Absolute, Clement [II: 263]

[15]

O ye who believe! When you contract a debt for a fixed term, record it in writing. Let a scribe record it in writing between you in [terms of] equity..... [II: 282]

[16]

Confound not truth with falsehood, nor knowingly conceal the truth [II: 42]

[17]

Say: Lo! My worship and my sacrifice and my living and my dying are for Allah, Lord of the Worlds. [VI: 162]

[18]

Fair in the eyes of men is the love of things they covet; women and sons, heaped up piles of gold and silver, horses branded [with their mark] and wealth of cattle and well tilled land. Such are the possessions of this world's life. But with Allah is the best of goals [to return to]. [III: 14]

[19]

Who hoard their wealth and enjoin avarice on others and hide that which Allah has bestowed upon them of His bounty. For such disbelievers, We prepare a shameful doom. [IV: 37]

[20]

And they ask thee what they ought to spend. Say: that which is superfluous...... [II: 219]

[21]

And Allah knoweth that which ye keep hidden and that which ye proclaim. [XVI: 19]

[22]

Know that worldly life is only play, and idle talk, and pageantry, and boasting among you and rivalry in respect of wealth and children. [LVII: 20]

[23]

Lo! Allah enjoineth justice and benevolence and giving to kinsfolk, and forbiddeth lewdness and abomination and offence. [XVI: 90]

[24]

Call unto the way of thy Lord with wisdom and fair exhortation, and reason with them in the better way. Lo! Thy Lord is best aware of him who strayeth from his way, and He is best aware of those who go aright. [XVI: 125]

[25]

Come not near the wealth of the orphan save with that which

is better till he come to strength; and keep the covenant. Lo! Of the covenant it will be asked. [XVII: 34]

[26]

Fill the measure when ye measure, and weigh with a right balance; that is meet, and better in the end. [XVII: 35]

[27]

Unto each nation have We given sacred rights which they are to perform: so let them not dispute with thee of the matter, but summon thou unto thou Lord. Lo! Thou indeed followest right guidance. [XXII: 67]

[28]

You are the best community that has been sent forth to mankind. You enjoin the right and forbid the wrong; and you have faith in Allah. [III: 110]

[29]

Say (O Muslims): We believe in Allah and that which is revealed unto us and that which was revealed unto Abraham, Ismael, and Isaac, and Jacob, and the tribes, and that which Moses and Jesus received and that which the Prophets received from their Lord. We make no distinction between any of them, and unto Him we have surrendered. [II: 136]

[30]

Lo! Allah loveth not such as are proud and boastful. [IV: 36]

Acknowledgement

I am indebted to all writers and publishers by whose writings and publications this book has been enriched. I would also like to express my gratitude and appreciation to the following institutions and individuals for their valuable help rendered to me during the course of writing this book.

Institutions

1. Indian Council of Social Science Research North Eastern Regional Centre, Nongthymmai, Shillong
2. District Library, Arts and Culture Department, Government of Meghalaya, East Garo Hills, William Nagar.
3. State Central Library, Meghalaya, Shillong
4. Seng Bhalang Islam Library, Attached to Laitumkhrah Mosque, Shillong

Individuals

1. Dr. K. A. Ahmed
2. Mr. L. Ritchil
3. Mr. A. H. Bhuyan
4. Mr. Abu Sufyian
5. Ms. Cerilla Khonglah
6. Mr. D. R. Michael Buam

I shall fail in my duty if I do not express my love and appreciation for Khan Muhammad Amir Hussain and Lam Sin Alom for taking my care and helping me when I was busy in collecting information and writing this book.

I am grateful to Janab Nusrat Ali Nasri for taking all the trouble for bringing out the book early and unhesitantly in the present form.

I am also thankful to Muhammad Adul Bari for painstakingly editing the Book.

William Nagar
18th April 2003

Muhammad
Hasibor Rahman

Some Basic Facts about Meghalaya

Date of creation .... 21st January 1972

Population (Census 2001) 23,06,069

Sex ratio .... 975 females per 1000 males

Muslim Population in 2000

a) Total (estimated) 83,487

b) Percentage 3.46

Area in Sq. Km. .... 22[illegible]

Capital .... Shillong

Official Language .... English

Major languages .... Khasi, Jaintia & Garo

Other spoken languages: .... Hindi, Bengali, Asamese, Nepali & Urdu

Legislature .... Unicameral (60seats)

Literacy rate (Census 2001) 63.31%

Important places:

Shillong, Cherapunjee, Barapani, Tura, Phulbari, William Nagar, Mendipathar, Nongpoh, Byrnihat, Nongstoin, Jowai, Dawki, Mahendaraganj and Baghmara

Major tourist spots:

Lady Hydari Park, Ward's Lake, Shillong Peak, Golf Course, Cherrapunjee, Mawsmai, Barapani, Nokrek, Balpakram, Mawsynram, Mawkyrwat, Mirjumlah and Dargah of Hadrat Shah Kamal

Primary occupation .... Agriculture

Chief agricultural products:

Rice, maize, potato, tomato, cotton, ginger, turmeric, betel nut, betel leaf, orange, banana, pineapple, jackfruit, bay leaf, black pepper, etc.

Famous mosque in Meghalaya:

Police Bazar (Thana Road), Garikhana, Laban and Laitumkhrah (Fire-Brigade) and Mir Jumlah

Chief mineral resources .... Uranium, Coal, & Limestone

Reputed Muslim run educational institutions:

Islamia School (1920), Umshyrpi College (1994)

University .... NEHU (1973)

Advent of Islam .... 1300 A. D.

First Khasi poet .... Sheikh Muhammad Amjad Ali

First Post graduate in Urdu in Meghalaya .... Sayeedullah Nongrum

First Muslim IPS of Meghalaya .... C. Z. Ghafoor Pariat

First Khasi Muslim lady .... Jummah Nongrum

Foreword

In the recent years a substantial number of books have been produced tracing the history of origin, settlement of the different tribes of Meghalaya and analyzing the process of their socio-economic and political growth and development. But there is lack of literature about the Muslims, the second largest minority community of the state. As a result one finds it difficult to obtain first hand knowledge of the socio-economic and political condition and historical background of the Muslims of Meghalaya. Mohammad Hasibor Rahman's work, Muslims in Meghalaya, would go a long way to overcome this drawback and to promote communal harmony, peace and mutual understanding between the Muslims and other communities of the state.

While tracing the history of the Muslim settlement in the hilly region of Meghalaya in his readable work, Mohammad Rahman has asserted that the Muslims and the hill tribes of the state had been co-existing peacefully for centuries as next-door neighbours and that the Muslims had been playing an important role in all spheres of development of the state. The author has painstakingly documented many of the Muslim religious and educational institutions and peeped into the Muslim socio-economic problems and exhorted them to seek solution of their problems within the parameters of their religious ideology in an interesting and enlightening manner. According to him, poor socio-economic status of the Meghala's or Meghalaya Muslims is mainly due to their educational backwardness and lack of knowledge and skill required for their socio-economic advancement. This is, undoubtedly, an authoritative work on the Muslims of Meghalaya. I wish the author and his book a success.

Shillong,
7th May 2003

Azizul Hoque Bhuyan
ASTC, Shillong

Prologue

Bismillahir Rahmanir Raheem

"O my Lord! expand for me my breast; and make my task easy for me; And remove the impediment from my speech, so that they may understand what I say"

[Al-Qur'an XX: 25-28]

The idea of writing this book came to my mind in 1995, the year in which I received a letter from Janab A. Ali, Assistant Editor of 'The Muslim & Arab Perspective' (MAP), an international magazine published from Jamia Nagar, New Delhi asking me to "contribute a short note about Muslims in Meghalaya." I responded positively and the article was published under the caption, 'Muslims in Meghalaya' in the MAP (Vol. 3, Issues 1 – 6, 1996).

In September 2000, I presented a copy of the 'Milli Gazette', a fortnightly publication, edited by Dr. Zafarul-Islam Khan, a Muslim scholar of internarional repute, to Janab Sayeedullah Nongrum, Ex-Member of Meghalaya Legislative Assembly with a request to subscribe to it. In course of our discussion he disclosed that he wanted someone to write a book about the Muslims of Meghalaya. This served as a reminder to me and I noted it silently.

Keeping this in mind I made a survey by visiting some libraries and bookstalls to find whether there are any book written on the Muslim minority of the state. I had not come across such a book in my search and this led me to decide taking up the task of writing of this book.

The book is divided into nine chapters. The first chapter is an endeavour to narrate the political and natural divisions of the region called Meghalaya and history of its creation in brief with a reference to the hill tribes living therein.

In the second chapter, an attempt is made to trace the history of the Muslim settlement in the three regions of Garo Hills, Khasi Hills and Jaintia Hills since the beginning of the thirteenth century A.D.

In chapter three, a brief study of the Muslim population in relation to other communities is made on the basis of available statistics for making references for the purpose.

The fourth chapter is a study into the nature of the contact and relationship of the Muslims with the different hill tribes in the light of their historical backgrounds.

In chapter five, the contribution of the Muslims in the different developmental programmes of the hill regions of the present day Meghalaya is discussed.

In the sixth chapter, it is attempted to describe the role the Muslims played in the growth and development of politics in the hills since the first quarter of the twentieth century A.D. and the nature of their representation in the state legislature and ministry.

The seventh chapter is an effort to gauge the extent of the Islamic influence on the life and culture of the tribal people of the state.

In chapter eight, an attempt is made to throw light on the Muslim economic situation in the hill state for developing an understanding the problems of the Muslims needing immediate attention of the community and the state government.

In chapter nine, the religious and educational institutions run by the Muslim community on its own initiative and efforts are compiled and presented district-wise for the sake of posterity.

In the Epilogue, suggestions on how the problems of the Muslims of the state can be solved through their own actions and efforts is discussed to some extent in the light of their religious ideology.

It is expected that the book would be of immense help to those who wish to understand the Muslim situation in Meghalaya and work for their socio-economic development.

CHAPTER I

Political profile of Meghalaya

Meghalaya is the twenty-first state of the Indian union. It is a mountainous plateau of great scenic beauty. It was carved out of Assam as an autonomous state in April 1970 and declared a full-fledged state on January 21, 1972. The state is consisted of the area of two erstwhile districts of Assam, namely, Garo Hills and United Khasi and Jaintia Hills. Its total geographical area is 22,429 square kilometers and population is 23,06,069 as per 2001 census. There are, at present, seven districts: (1) West Garo Hills, (2) East Garo Hills, (3) South Garo Hills, (4) West Khasi Hills, (5) East Khasi Hills, (6) Jaintia Hills and (7) Ri Bhoi. Their headquarters are Tura, William Nagar, Baghmara, Nongstoin, Shillong, Jowai, and Nongpoh respectively (See Plate 1).

Location and boundary

Meghalaya is situated between 25°47= to 26° 10=N latitude and 89°45= to 92°45=E longitude. It is bounded on the north and the east by Assam, on the west by Assam and Bangladesh and on the south by Bangladesh. The state may be divided into three regions — Jaintia Hills in the east, Khasi Hills in the middle and Garo Hills in the west.

The Khasi Hills and the Jaintia Hills lie between the

Brahmaputra valley and the Barak valley. The Khasi Hills is bounded on the north by Kamrup and Nowgong districts of Assam, on the east by North Cachar and Karbi Anglong district of Assam, on the south by Sylhet district of Bangladesh and on the west by Garo hills. It has a geographical area of 10,542 square kilometers.

The Jaintia Hills is bounded on the north by Karbi Anglong district and on the east by Cachar district of Assam, on the south by Sylhet district of Bangladesh and on the west by the Khasi Hills. It has an area of 3,863 square kilometers.

The Garo Hills is located in the southwestern corner of the present state of Meghalaya. It has a geographical area of 8,083 square kilometers bounded by Goalpara district of Assam on the north, by the Khasi Hills on the east, by Mymensing district of Bangladesh on the south and by Rangpur district of Bangladesh and Goalpara district of Assam on the west.

People

The Khasis and the Syntengs belong to the Mon-Khmer branch of the Austric family and the Garos to the Tibeto-Burman race in origin. It is difficult to trace the history of their settlement in this region of India due to lack of reliable historical evidences.

The Khasi Hills is predominately inhabited by the Khasi, the Bhoi and the War people, the Jaintia Hills by the Jaintias who are also called Syntengs or Pnars and the Garo Hills by the Garo people. In 1872, the total Khasi and Jaintia population was 1,40,356. It increased to 1,67,804 in1881,

1,97,904 in1891 and 2,02, 250 in 1901. As per 1901 census, the population of the Khasi Hills and the Jaintia Hills was 1, 34, 329, and 67, 921 respectively. Out of this, 1,07,800 persons were Khasis, 47,900 Jaintias and 12,800 Mikirs.[1] It seems that the rest were Hindus, Muslims, Christians, and others.

Muslims appeared in the Khasi-Jaintia Hills long before the advent of the Christians. They were quite visible in the different parts of the hills by 1600 A.D. As per 1901 census 88 per cent of the hills population were adherents of the tribal religions, 3 per cent were Hindus and remaining 9 per cent were Christians and Muslims.

It appears that the Khasis and the Jaintias used to raid the villages in the plains at the end of the eighteenth century. Captain R. B. Pemberton recorded their raids in his 'Report on the eastern frontier of British India' (Calcutta 1835) thus: " They descended into the plains both of Assam and Sylhet, and ravaged with fire and sword the villages which stretched along the base of this lofty region. Night was the time almost invariably chosen for these murderous assaults, when neither sex nor age was spared."[2]

The total population of the Garo Hills was 1,21,570 in 1891 and 1,38, 274 in 1901. In 1901, 82 per cent of the Garo Hills population were the followers of animistic beliefs, 10 per cent were Hindus and 6 per cent were Muslims. A total of 3,629 persons were natives Christians.[3]

The Garos were also in the habit of raiding the plains of Bengal and head hunting. During the period from May 1857 to October 1859, they raided Goalpara nine times and took away twenty heads.[4] "The exactions levied by the subordinates of these border chiefs irritated the hill men, and the belief that the spirits of their headmen required the souls of others to attend them in the next world acted as a further incitement to the dispatch of the raiding parties."[5]

The British annexation of the hills

The United Khasi and Jaintia Hills was neither a part of Bengal during the Muslim rule in Bengal[6] nor of Assam during the Ahom rule (1236—1826 A.D.) in Assam.[7] The Khasis and the Jaintias were independents and ruled by themselves. They had keen interest in trade and commerce. The Garo Hills formed the part of the Muslim ruled Bengal.

The Burmese invaded Assam in1817 A.D. at the invitation of Badan Chandra Barphukan. Then King Purander Singh invited the British to drive out the Burmese invaders from Assam. The British defeated the Burmese in the war and concluded a treaty with them on February 24, 1826. The treaty is known as the Treaty of Yandabu in the history of Assam. By the treaty, the Burmese ceded Assam to the British. Mr. David Scott (1823—1831 A.D.), the Commissioner of Rangpur, was appointed to administer the new territory.

After the treaty of Yandabu, the British gradually took over the Khasi Hills, the Jaintia Hills and the Garo Hills. In 1826 David Scott made an arrangement with the Khasi kings for construction of a road from Assam to Sylhet through their territories for the purpose of establishing communication link between the Brahmaputra valley and the Surma valley. The construction work of the road was started. Around this time a Bengali chaprasi announced that the hill areas would be brought under taxation. Alarmed by this announcement, the Khasis revolted against the British and killed their two officers along with their sixty workers.[8] Military operation was started at once but revolt continued. On April 4, 1829, U. Tirot Singh, the king of Nongkhlow declared war against the British. But in 1833 he was captured and sent to Dhaka. On July17, 1835 he died in the British captivity in Dhaka.

The British took possession of the Jaintia Hills and the Jaintia kingdom in the plains (now in Bangladesh) in 1835 for kidnapping three British subjects and sacrificing them to the goddess Kali.[9] U Kiang Nongbah revolted against the British in 1862, but was not successful to free the Jaintia land from the British yoke.[10]

The Garos came into contact with the British as far back as in 1765 A.D. when the East India Company acquired Rangpur from the Mughals. During the Mughal rule the Hindu Zamindars were allowed to hold a number of estates at the foot of the Garo Hills. These estates included many Garo villages. In return, these Zamindars paid tribute to the Mughal Foujdar of Rangamati in the form of elephant and a small quantity of Aghar wood.[11] The Muslim contact with the Garos was started with the establishment of their rule in Bengal.

David Scott was posted in Rangpur in 1812 as the Judge Magistrate of the district. In 1822 he was made Civil Commissioner of the north-eastern parts of Rangpur. At this time it was found that the Hindu Zamindars exploited the Garos economically and the Garos conducted raids in the plains. "The chiefs or Zamindars of the marches were expected to restrain their incursions, but soon it was found that their tyranny and exactions were the chief cause of the raids"[12] To solve this problem, David Scott recommended for separation of Garo Hills from Rangpur. Following this a new district consisting of Goalpara, Karaibari, Garo Hills and Dhubri was created and Scott was made its Commissioner.

In 1866, Lieutenant Williamson was posted in Garo Hills as its administrator and the Garo Hills was brought under the British rule following a raid conducted into Mymensing by the Garos. In1869 Garo hills was made a separate district with its headquarter at Tura.[13] In 1870 a survey of the hills was carried out. The Garos seized a coolie of the survey team. In 1872 an expedition was dispatched through the independent territories of Garo Hills district.[14] Togan N. Sangma, a freedom loving Garo man, resisted the British expedition at Rongrenggre but he was captured and hanged at Sisobibra on December12, 1872.

The British administrative headquarter of the Khasi and Jaintia Hills was set up in Cherrapunji in 1834. Later on, it was transferred to Shillong from Cherrapunji in 1866 because of incessant rain. In 1874 a province of Assam was constituted under a Chief Commissioner and the Khasi Hills, the Jaintia Hills, the Garo Hills and the Bengal districts of Goalpara, Cachar and Sylhet were incorporated in it. Shillong was made the capital of the new province and remained so till January 1974.

The British ruled the hill region of present Meghalaya over a century. During the period, they developed communication by constructing roads and bridges, and agriculture by introducing cultivation of new crops, vegetables and fruits in the hills. The Christian missionaries established a number of educational institutions and dispensaries in the hills and developed tribal languages and literatures.

Accession of the Hills to Indian union

There were twenty-five small states in the Khasi and Jaintia Hills. The chief of each of the states was called Syiem. On August 22, 1946, all the Syiems joined together and formed an organization called 'The Khasi States Federation.' By the end of 1947, except Syiem of Nongstoin, all the Syiems of the Khasi states signed the 'Instrument of Accession' and joined the Indian union. "The Syiem of Nongstoin wanted time to make his option between joining India or Pakistan since his state has a long boundary with East Pakistan on which it depended for its food stuff and essential commodities and to which it sold its agricultural products and other products like boulder, timber etc."[15] However, after initial hesitation he too signed the 'Instrument of Accession' and joined Indian union.

The credit for getting all the Syiems to sign the Instrument of Accession goes to Akbar Hydari, the then governor of Assam. However, when governor Hydari requested the Khasi states to sign the merger agreement, they refused to sign it "on the ground that they had no authority to do so."[16]

Reason for joining India

After the independence of India, the Khasi-Jaintia Hills and the Garo Hills were divided into two separate districts and included in the state of Assam. The hill people of these districts had decided to join India because of the fact that the constitution of India has granted them all necessary protection in the matter of their land, religion, language, culture and custom. They are also given the right to govern themselves through the institution of Autonomous District Council, to protect their own interests and to develop themselves according to their own wishes and will.

Demand for separate state

Despite all these constitutional concessions and safeguards, the hill people began to feel insecure about their future in Assam within a year of the enforcement of the Indian constitution. Between 1951 and 1952 the Assam ministry headed by Shri Bishnuram Medhi took a decision to give the non-tribal government servants and others permanent land settlement in the heart of Shillong town. Sensing the unhappiness of the tribal on the issue of the land settlement, Mr. Abdul Matlib Mazumdar, a senior minister in the Medhi cabinet opposed the cabinet decision on the land settlement and warned: "You have been playing with their (Khasi tribals) women, they were quiet. You have taken their jobs, they were keeping quiet. But once you touched their land, they will revolt and hit back."[17] But the timely warning of Mr. Mazumdar went unheeded. The Assam government went ahead with its decision to allot tribal land to the non-tribals. Within a year, forcast of Mr. Mazumdar turned into reality. The demand for separate state for tribal people was raised.

While examining the factors that led the hill people to raise the demand for separate state an acknowledged authority on the north-east India observed: "The average tribal was no more competent to read the constitution than was the Indian villager elsewhere. But he had eyes to see vast tracts of the most valuable land in the hill capital of Shillong being allotted to Assamese, Bengalis and other non-tribals despite all the safeguards of the constitution."[18]

Moreover, after the independence of India, the tribal people had lost the faith they had in the institution of the governor during the British rule. "During the British period, the governor did in fact govern. Even in the 'partially excluded' hill areas, while it was open to ministers to offer advice, the final decision lay with the governor, who knew his rights and was not afraid of exercising them. The hill tribal did not in fact even feel the need for constitutional protection, as he had complete and unqualified confidence in the governor and knew he was in safe hands. Although the new constitution also vested the governor with discretionary powers, there were few governors of the stature and strength of mind to exercise such powers against the advice or wishes of their ministers. Sir Akbar Hydari was the last of the governors of Assam to effectively govern and even where he was constitutionally bound by and acted on the advice of ministers he succeeded in projecting the impression that his was the deciding voice. He was thus able to retain the confidence of the tribal people, and had he lived, he might have contained them for some further time within Assam. But no organization can or should depend on the personality of the individual and after his passing away, the tribals soon came to realize that whatever the constitutional safeguards, ultimate authority lay not with governor but with elected ministers and that, as long as the tribals remained within Assam, their future destiny lay in the hands of the Assamese."[19] Sir Hydari was governor of Assam from May 4, 1947 to December 28, 1948.

Hill state Movement

On July 6, 1960, the political parties of the two districts of Garo Hills and Khasi-Jaintia Hills formed an All Party Hill Leaders' Conference (APHLC) for achieving their objective of separate state. In 1962, the Assam Legislative Assembly passed the Official Language Act making Assamese the official language of the.state. The hill people saw the Act as a direct threat to their language, culture and identity. The APHLC carried out its movement through strikes and demonstrations which reached its peak in September 1968.[20] The non-tribals including the Muslims of the two hill districts also extended their support to the movement for the hill state. "One single incident could mould the minority communities of the hills towards the reorganization of Assam. It was the large scale acts of violence, looting and arson against the non-Assamese minority communities, the *Marwaris* in particular, and the desecration of the National Flag on the Republic Day of 1968 (at Guwahati) with a cry, Assam for Assamese."[21] The hill leaders assured the minority communities that their all legitimate rights and interests would be safeguarded in the new hill state. "English would be the official language of the state. The legitimate interests of the minorities would be protected. The state would guarantee equality of opportunity"[22] to all communities.

Creation of hill state

In September1968, the government of India declared that

an Autonomous hill state within Assam would be created. Thus the demand for separate state for the hill people was fulfilled under the State Reorganization Act of 1971. The name of the new hill state is given Meghalaya meaning 'Abode of Clouds'.

Expectations and responsibilities

A minister of the new state of Meghalaya outlined the expectations and responsibilities of the people of his state in these words: "Now that we have our own state, the way is clear for an efficient, clean government that will really help the people and bring please drop 'to" them prosperity and happiness. No more corruption, no more red tape and dilly–dallying; we tribals are practical people who believe in work more than words; we shall settle all our problems on the spot and not waste time scribbling on office files. Meghalaya will be an example to the rest of India of how an efficient state should be run."[23]

Conclusion

Since the creation of Meghalaya, thirty years has elapsed. During the period the state has made a good progress in all sectors of development particularly in the field of health, education, agriculture, rural electrification, supply of safe drinking water, road and telephone communications and banking, but it is still to go a long way to fulfill the hopes and aspirations of the people generated at the time of creation of the new state. Over 50 per cent of the population still lives below the poverty line. However the future of the state is not bleak.

ENDNOTES

1. B.C. Allen [Henceforth BCA], E.A. Gait [EAG], H.F. Howword [HFH] and C.G.H. Allen [CGHA]. Gazetteer of Bengal and North-East India, 2001, Mittal Publications, A—110, Mohan Garden, New Delhi- 110059, pp. 484—85.
2. Ibid, p. 483.
3. Ibid, p. 503.
4. Ibid
5. Ibid, p. 502.
6. Ibid, p. 420.
7. Das A.K., Assam's Agony, 1982, Lancers Publications, New Delhi- 110048, p. 256.
8. BCA, EAG, HFH & CGHA, Op.cit. p. 483.
9. Ibid, p. 420.
10. [L] Rymbai R.T. [Rtd. IAS], Integration of the Khasi states: The untold history, Souvenir, Khasi Students' Union, 20th Anniversary Celebration, 1978—1998, Edited by Paul Lyngdoh, p. 63.
11. Mackenzie A., A history of relations of the government with the hill tribes of North-East frontier of Bengal, 1884, p.245.
12. Gait Edward, A history of Assam, 1984, LBS Publications, Gauhati, Assam, p. 317.
13. Ibid.
14. BCA, HFH, & CGHA, Op. cit., pp. 32 & 503.
15. [L] Rymbai R.T. Op. cit. p. 64.
16. Rao V.V., Pakem B., Hazarika N., A century of government and politics in North-East India, Vol. II, [Meghalaya], 1984, S. Chand and Company Ltd., New Delhi—110065, p. 34.
17. Mazumdar Abdul Muhim, Abdul Matlib Mazumdar: Birth Centenary tributes [1890 —1990] Edited by Anwaruddin Chowdhury, p. 12.
18. Rustomji Nari, Imperilled Frontiers: India's North-Eastern Border lands, 1983, Oxford University Press, New Delhi-110002, p. 81.
19. Ibid, p. 82.
20. Meghalaya District Gazetteer: Jaintia Hills, 1996, Edited by Simon I. M., Directorate of Arts and Culture, Government of Meghalaya, Shillong, pp. 27—28.
21. Kar P.C., Glimses of the Garos, 1982, Garo Hills Book Emporium, Tura, West Garo Hills, pp. 276—277.
22. Rao V. V., Pakem B, Hazarika N., Op. cit., P. 42.
23. Quoted in Rustomji Nari, Op. cit., P. 84.

CHAPTER II

History of the Muslim Settlement

The history of the Muslim settlement in Meghalaya can be traced from the beginning of the 13th century A.D. The population of the plain region of East Bengal bordering the Garo Hills, the Khasi Hills and the Jaintia Hills was comprised of the Koches, the Meches, the Tharus, the Ravas, the Hajongs, the Garos, the Khasis and the different Hindu lower castes. A large number of people of these communities had converted to Islam.[1] Many of these converts settled at the foot of the hills, particulary of the Garo and Jaintia Hills and took up agriculture and business as their profession. A chief of the Mech community came into the fold of Islam and became known as Ali Mech. He preached his new religion among the local tribes and converted many of them to Islam.

In 1198 Muhammad Ibn Bakhtiyar Khilji conquered Bengal by overthrowing its last king Lakshman Sen and established his capital at Gour. In 1206 he launched an expedition to conquer Tibet through a country inhabited by Koch, Mech and Tharu tribes. He took Ali Mech with him as his guide. On reaching Kamrup, he found himself besieged by the army of the Kamrup king. However, he managed to find his way to Deocot in the south of Dinajpur with the help of the Mech inhabitants.[2] But he left behind most of his soldiers who chose to settle in Assam rather then to go back with their defeated general. According to his *Safarnamah* (*Torbat Nazzar*), Ibn Battuta saw people having similarity with Turkish people in Assam during his visit to the country in 1346. It may be that people whom he saw were the descendants of the Turkish soldiers who came to Kamrup in 1206 and to Darrang in the 8th century from China crossing over the Himalaya and settled there.

According to Baharistan-e-Gaibi, during the reign of emperor Jahangir (1605 – 1627), the Muslim ruler of Bengal invaded the Cachari kingdom twice. The first invasion took place when Islam Khan was the governor of Bengal. In 1612 Qasim Khan succeeded his brother Islam Khan. The second invasion was made during Qasim Khan's governorship. The Mughal army defeated the Cacharis and conquered Asurakriti and Protapgarh. "In the account of this expedition mention is made of the Khasis as a tribe living in the Cachari frontier, and also of a tribe calling themselves Mughals, who claimed to be the descendants of soldiers left in-charge of the country by Timur after he had conquered it."[3]

Pre-British period

During the period from 1206 to 1667, the Muslim rulers of Bengal invaded Assam more than seventeen times. During this period a number of Muslim saints and traders migrated to Assam. The Ahom monarchs brought many Muslim artisans and learned men from Bengal. The Muslim soldiers, who were left behind or taken as prisoners of war by the different kings of Assam, had settled in different places of Assam after their release.

Since 1662 Goalpara that included Garo Hills was under the Muslim rulers of Bengal till 1765. Garo Hills was not unknown region to the Muslims. Some Muslim saints like Shah Kamal visited the hill areas adjacent to the plains of Bengal and Assam and preached Islam among the local inhabitants. As a result a good number of hill people embraced Islam impressed by its teaching and simplicity. The majority of Muslim population of Meghalaya is, therefore, found today concentrated mainly at the western foot of the Garo Hills.

The legend has it that while going back to Bengal in 1663 after conquering the whole of Assam, Mir Jumlah, the great general of Mughal emperor Aurangzeb, halted at a hilltop located at the foot of Garo hills near Mankachar for some days for taking rest as he was tired and sick It appears that the Muslim settlement in the plains tract of Garo Hills took place long before the visit of Mir Jumlah.

The Khasi Hills had a long border with East Bengal and Assam. Some Muslims from the plains of neighbouring districts of Assam and Bengal used to visit the hills in search of employment and business opportunities. A few of them married Khasi women and run their business in the hills. Some Khasi kings employed Muslims and honoured them with high office like chieftainship.[4] Every Khasi chief appointed Bengali agents called *Duardars* to keep accounts and arrange negotiations and contracts with the Mughal authorities and traders while lease holders employed Bengali workmen in mines.[5] "Jainarayan (1698-1731), the Raja of Jaintia on the request of the prominent Muslims in the state brought a learnt Muslim scholar from Hardwar for religious leadership of his Muslim subjects."[6]

It appears that Jaintia settlement was extended to the Gangetic plains of Sylhet long after the Muslim settlement was began there. The district of Sylhet was once divided into three petty kingdoms — Gour, Lour and Jaintia. Sikandar Khan Gazi, nephew of Sultan Ala-uddin (1296-1316), and Shah Jalal conquered Gour or Sylhet proper in 1303 in the reign of Firuz Shah in Bengal.[7] Shah Jalal was a Muslim saint. He was settled down in Sylhet and preached Islam there among the people of different aboriginal races. "Sylhet had a settled Muslim population even before its conquest by Shah Jalal. The last Hindu ruler of the Lour kingdom had embraced Islam and that naturally inspired further Muslim settlement there."[8] Govind was the name of the ruler of Lour[9]. In 1500 Jaintia king Parbat Ray "extended the sway of the Jaintia kings into the plains tract at the foot of his ancestoral kingdom in the hills."[10] The Muslim rulers of Bengal did not conquer the hill kingdom. However, "....The Muslim population in the plains division of Jayantia considerably increased during the period (of Mughal rule) and Raja of Jayantia had to appoint Qazi for the administration of justice among their Muslim subjects."[11] In 1901, 53 per cent of the total population of Sylhet district was Muslims.

British Period

During the British rule many Muslims along with Bengali

Hindus were brought to the Khasi-Jaintia Hills and the Garo Hills to assist the newly established administration at different occasions. For the construction of Shillong-Sylhet Road via Dawki, Shillong-Guwahati Road and Shillong–Silchar Road via Jowai, Muslim (and Hindu) contractors, businessmen and labourers were hired from Bengal. After annexing the Khasi-Jaintia states into their rule, the British made Charrapunji their headquarter for the of purpose of running the administration of the hill region and probably posted some Muslim officials, both civil and military, there to assist them. Some Muslim traders were also brought from as far as Calcutta.

Cherrapunji is located about 55 kilometres away from Shillong on a plateau that is overlooking the plains of Sylhet from 1358 metres above the sea level. It is the place of highest rainfall in the world and an important centre of Khasi Hills. Many Muslim traders from Sylhet used to visit the market before the independence of India.

After Shillong was made capital of the province of Assam and road transport improved, a number of Muslims of different professional backgrounds migrated to Shillong from Kabul, Sylhet, Dhaka, Calcutta, Guwahati, Goalpara, Bihar, Punjab and many other places of northen India and settled down there for trade and employment. Some of them married tribal women after converting them to their religion. Shillong is situated at a distance of 100 kilometres from Guwahati at an altitude of 1496 metres above the sea level. "According to the Khasi legend, it derives its name from the word, 'Shulong', the creator, who once upon a time born to a Khasi peasant girl"[12] The first Muslim settlement in Shillong took place in sixteenth century.

As many as four Muslims were witnesses to the Recognizance Agreement singed by Oophar Rajah of Bhawul Poonjee before captain Townshend at Cherrapoonji in 1832. While three of the witnesses were *Duardars*, one was the resident of parganah Mahram, Mouza Nolegong (See Appendix B). This points out that the Muslim settlement took place in Khasi Hills long before the advent of the British and Muslims were enjoying a respectable position in the Khasi society.

Jummah Nongrum, daughter of a Pathan from Kabul and Mrs. Donman Nongrum, of Laban locality of Shillong claimed to be the first Muslim Khasi lady.[13] Her father migrated to Shillong in the last part of the 19th century and married her mother in 1900. Sayeedullah Nongrum, a prominent Muslim citizen of Shillong claims his descent from Jummah Nongrum.

With the separation of Garo hills from Goalpara in 1869 and establishment of its headquarter at Tura, there was a drop of the Muslim population in the hills as some Muslim inhabited plain areas of the district went under Goalpara district. However, a good number of Muslims migrated from Goalpara, Rangpur, Dhaka etc. to Tura as the new district provided new scopes of employment and business for the outsiders. Some of them married Garo women and settled down in Tura. Some Muslims from as far as Afghanistan and central India also settled in different places of Garo hills for business purposes. As per 1901 census, six per cent of the total population of Garo Hills was Muslim.

The Muslim population of the hill region of the Garo Hills and Khasi-Jaintia Hills was consisted of Assamese, Bengali, Hindi, Urdu, Khasi and Nepali speaking people. Occupationally, they were cultivators, government servants, traders, builders, contractors, tea planters, jewelers, tailors, bakers, washer men, butchers, barbers, shoe makers and the like.

Post independence period

During the British period, the Muslims had migrated from Bengal to the hills, but their number was very small in comparison to the Hindus. After independence of India their migration to the hill region was stopped. On the other hand, many pre-independence Muslim migrants returned to the place of their origin. With the transfer of Sylhet along with Jaintiapur to East Pakistan (now Bangladesh) in 1947, the Muslim population in Jaintia Hills became very insignificant. Their number in the capital town of Shillong was 3026 in 1941. It was reduced to 2418 in 1951, while the population of other religious groups like Hindus and Christians generously increased.

Places of Muslim settlement

In East Khasi Hills district Muslim population is found mainly in the state capital of Shillong. They are scattering in the localities like Laban, Bishnupur, Police Bazar, Garikhana, Mawprem, Barapather, Jhalupara and Laitumkhrah. In Ri Bhoi district settled Muslim population is found in Byrnihat on the Assam-Meghalaya border. A small number of Muslims has also been living in Umden and Nongpoh. In the district of Jaintia Hills a very few Muslims are found scattering in Ladrymbai, Khliehriat, Sonapur, Umkiang, Muktapur, Jowai and Dawki.

Majority of Muslims of Meghalaya have been living in Garo Hills. The district of West Garo Hills has settled Muslim population in Mahendraganj, Kalaichar, Sobribari, Kasaripara, Rajabala, Bhaibari, Phulbari, Bholarbhita, Tura, Rangapani and other places on the Assam – Meghalaya border.

Deportation of Muslims to East Pakistan

During the period after independence of India and before the creation of Meghalaya, a good number of Muslims were detected and deported either as anti-national or undesirable element or East Pakistani from the different Places of the Garo Hills. After the creation of Bangladesh, Muslim Indians, particularly those who are uneducated and poor, living in the state are being duped as Bangladeshis, while real foreigners belonging to different non-Muslim communities are allowed to settle and live in the state without any hindrance.

Migration of Muslims to Assam

Within a decade of creation of Meghalaya, minority communities, who had supported the movement for the creation of a separate state wholeheartedly and opted to live with their tribal brothers and sisters in the state, started to feel insecure. The slogan of tolerance, peace, unity, equality and development began to evaporate in the air. The seed of corruption, intolerance, communal hatred and insurgency was sowed. As a result a good number of Muslims along with the members of other minority communities migrated to Assam, Bengal and other Indian states mainly from Shillong and Tura after selling their land and houses for the safety and security of their lives and honour. During and after the horror of communal riots of 1987 in Garo Hills, many Muslims migrated from Tura, William Nagar, Rongjeng and other places to Assam for the security of their lives.

Conclusion

After independence of India, the Garo Hills and the Khasi-Jaintia Hills have been included in the sixth schedule of the Indian constitution. The non-tribal citizens are debarred from acquiring land in their names after the creation of the state and those among them who have been already owning and possessing landed property are not legally permitted to sell and transfer their land to other non-tribals or to their descendents except to tribals. Muslim settlement remained confined to only few pockets of the states. Many early Muslim settlers of the hills have lost their identity and assimilated into the tribal life and culture along with their descendents because of long association with the hill tribes and their isolation from their own community.

ENDNOTES

1. BCA, RAG, HFH & CGHA, Gazetteer of Bengal & North-East India, 2001, Mittal Publications, A—110, Mohan Garden, New Delhi—11005, pp. 265 &325.

2. Gait Edward, A history of Assam, 1984, LBS Publications, Guwahati Assam, p. 36, Tabaqat-e-Nasiri, (Revrty's translation) Vol. 1, P. 560, Riyaz-us-Salatin (Abdus Salam's translation) PP. 62 to 68.

3. Ibid, P. 253

4. Mathur P.R.G., The Khasi of Meghalaya, 1979, Cosmo Publications, New Delhi, p. 42.

5. Dutta P. N., Relations of the Khasis and Jaintias with their southern neighbours till the British Intervention, Paper presented in the First session of North-East India History Association, Shillong, 1980 quoted in Dutta Sushil Chandra, The North-East and Mughals (1661—1714), 1984, D. K. Publications, 29 / 9, Nangia park, Shakti Nagar, Delhi—110007, P. 222.

6. Ali S.M., The History of Jaintia, P.31, quoted in Dutta Sushil Chandra, The North-East and Mughals (1661-1714), 1984, D.K. Publications, Nangia Park, Shakti Nagar, Delhi-110007, P. 244.

7. Gait Edward, Op. Cit. P.276, Dr. Wise in the Journal of Asiatic Society of Bengal, 1873, P. 278, Waldar Nasiruddin, Suhel-e-Yemen 1860, The J.A.S.B., 1922, P. 43.

8. Kar M., Muslims in Assam politics, 1997, Vikas Publishing House Pvt. Ltd., 576 Masjid Road, Jangpura, New Delhi—110014, pp. 1—2.

9. Gait Edward, Op. Cit., P 277.

10. Ibid, P. 261.

11. Dutta sushil Chandra, The North-East and the Mughals, (1661—1714), 1984, D.K. Publications, 29/9, Nangia Park, Shakti Nagar, Delhi—110007, p. 219.

12. Rahman Mohammad Hasibor, Muslims in Shillong, The Milli Gazette, New Delhi, Vol. 2, No.19, 1—15 October, 2001, P. 6.

13. Mathur P. R. G., Op. Cit., P. 44.

CHAPTER III

Muslim demography

The population of Meghalaya has increased to 23,06,069 in 2001 from 3,40,524 in 1901. It is composed of the Khasis, the Jaintias, the Garos, the Hindus, the Muslims, the Koches, the Hajongs, the Ravas, the Dalus, the Jains, the Sikhs and the Buddhists. However, its " Principal inhabitants are the Garos, the Khasis and the Jaintias."[1] Over 64 per cent of them have already been converted to Christianity. Table 1 reflects the population growth trend of Meghalaya in the last one century.

Population growth of Meghalaya

The low population growth rate during the British period was due to high rate of morbidity and mortality among people caused by the diseases like malaria, cholera and kala-azar. After the independence of India, population growth has shown an increasing trend with the reduction of death rate and increase in the life expectancy as a consequence of improvement of health infrastructure, literacy rate and standard of living. The reason of low growth of population during 1941-1951 is due to migration of people from the state at the time of independence and transfer of Jaintiapur to East Pakistan.

Table 1: Population Growth of Meghalaya (1901-2001)

Census year	Total population	Percentage of growth
1901	3,40,524	—
1911	3,90,005	15.71
1921	4,22,403	7.21
1931	4,80,837	13.83
1941	5,55,820	15.59
1951	6,05,674	8.97
1961	7,69,380	27.03
1971	10,11,699	31.50
1981	13,35,819	32.30
1991	17,74,778	31.80
2001	23,06,069	29.94

District wise-population

Among the seven districts of Meghalaya, East Khasi Hills is the most populous district while South Garo Hills is the most thinly populated one. A glimpse of the population of all districts in the state can be had from Table 2.

Religion-wise population

According to national census report, the main religious groups of Meghalaya are Christian, the Hindu, the Muslim, the Buddhist, the Jain and the Sikh. Their numbers and percentage to the state's total population are shown in Table 3.

Table 2: District area and population (1991—2001)

Districts	Area in sq. kms.	Population 1991	Population 2001
East Khasi Hills	2798	5,37,906	6,60,995
West Khasi Hills	5247	2,20,157	2,94,195
Ri Bhoi	2448	1,27,312	1,92,795
Jaintia Hills	3819	2,20,473	2,95,692
West Garo Hills	3714	4,03,027	5,15,813
East Garo Hills	2603	1,88,830	2,47,554
South Garo Hills	1850	77,073	99,105
Meghalaya	**22429**	**17,74,778**	**23,06,069**

Table 3: Meghalaya Population by religion (1961—1991)

Religion	Population - 1961		Population – 1971		Population - 1991	
	Number	%	Number	%	Number	%
Christians	2,70,912	35.21	4,75,267	46.98	11,46,092	64.58
Hindus	1,40,445	18.26	1,87,144	18.50	2,60,960	14.67
Muslims	23,019	2.99	26,347	2.60	61,462	3.46
Sikhs	1,333	0.17	1,262	0.12	2,612	0.15
Buddhists	1,011	0.13	1,878	0.19	2,934	0.16
Jains	129	0.02	268	0.63	445	0.02
Others	3,22,912	41.97	3,18,168	31.45	2,98,466	16.82
Not stated	9,619	1.25	1,369	0.13	2,461	0.14
Total	**7,69,380**	**100.00**	**10,11,699**	**100.00**	**17,74,778**	**100.00**

The district-wise proportion of population of major religious groups of Meghalaya as reflected in 1991 census is given in Table 4.

Table 4: District-wise percentage of major religious groups (1991)

District	Hindus	Muslims	Christians	Others
East Khasi Hills	20.07	1.20	60.40	18.31
East Garo Hills	6.20	0 .63	80.74	12.43
Jaintia Hills	4.47	0.32	62.72	32.49
West Khasi Hills	2.07	0.08	90.34	7.53
West Garo Hills	20.96	10.69	53.03	15.31
Total	**14.67**	**3.46**	**64.58**	**17.29**

Muslim population

The Muslims are the second largest religious minority community in Meghalaya the Hindus being the largest minority group. Out of the state's total population of 7,69,380 in 1961, 10,11,699 in 1971, 13,35,819 in 1981, and 17,74,778 in 1991, the Muslim population was 23,019, 26,347, 41,434 and 61,462 respectively. Their percentage to the total population of the state rose from 2.99 in 1961 to 3.46 in 1991. The growth of the Muslim population in the state is shown in the Table 5.

Table 5: Growth of Muslim Population in Meghalaya (1961-1991)

Year	Total Population	Muslim Population	Percentage of Muslims to total population
1961	7,69,380	23,019	2.99
1971	10,11.699	26,347	2.60
1981	13,35,819	41,434	3.10
1991	**17,74,788**	**61, 462**	**3.46**

The growth of the Muslim population is more or less constant. Muslim concentration is the highest in West Garo Hills followed by East Khasi Hills, East Garo Hills, Jaintia Hills and West Khasi Hills. While majority of the Muslims of West Garo Hills live in the rural areas, almost all the Muslims of other districts live in the urban areas.

Table 6: District-wise distribution of Muslim population of Meghalaya (1991)

District	Total Population	Muslim Population	Percentage of Muslims to total population
Jaintia Hills	2,20,473	722	0.32
East Khasi Hills	6,65,218	8043	1.20
West Khasi Hills	2,20,157	182	0.08
East Garo Hills	1,88,830	1185	0.63
West Garo Hills	4,80,100	51,330	10.69
Total	**17,74,778**	**61,462**	**3.46**

The estimated Muslim population[2] during the period from 1997 to 2000 along with their percentage to the total population of the state is given in Table 7.

Table 7: Estimated Muslim Population (1997-2000)

Year	Muslim population	Muslim percentage
1997	77,768	3.69
1998	80,879	3.73
1999	80,980	3.64
2000	83,487	3.64

Muslim linguistic groups. The Muslim population of the state is composed of Bengali, Assamese, Hindi, Nepali, Urdu, Khasi, and Jaintia speaking people. However, most of the Muslims speak Bengali. Table 8 shows the population of different linguistic groups of Meghalaya. The statistics on the various linguistic groups of the Muslims are not separately available.

Table 8: Population in Meghalaya by mother tongue (1961—1971)

Languages by mother tongue	Population		Percentage of increase / decrease
	1961	1971	
Assamese	26,338	23,410	- 11.12
Bengali	52,986	93,967	+77.34
Hindi	9,541	17,220	+80.48
Nepali	32,284	44,445	+37.67
Garo	2,51,472	3,28,613	+30.67
Khasi (and Jaintia)	3,45,550	4,57,064	+32.27
Others	51,209	46,980	+8.26
Total	7,69,380	10,11,699	+31.50

Source: (Census 1961—1971, social and cultural tables, India)

While the Assamese speaking people during 1961-1971 were decreased by 11.12 per cent, Bengali, Hindi and Nepali speaking people were increased by 77.34 per-cent, 80.48 percent and 37.67 per cent respectively. Since the growth of the Muslim Population during the decade was normal, most of the speakers of Bengali, Hindi and Nepali were Hindus and their increase was due to migration into the state from outside.

In the 1971 census report, 66,871 persons were shown to be belonging to different non-tribal language speaking groups in Garo Hills. This is reflected in Table 9.[3]

Table 9: Non-tribal linguistic groups in Garo Hills (1971)

Linguistic group / mother tongue	Total	Males	Females
Assamese	3,472	5,246	4,226
Bengali	53,485	22,122	25,363
Gujrati	2	2	—
Hindi	3,617	2,524	1,093
Kashmiri	10	6	4
Malayalam	33	24	9
Marathi	7	6	1
Oriya	45	42	3
Punjabi	52	36	16
Tamil	4	1	3
Telegu	58	55	3
Urdu	86	82	4
Total	**66,871**	**36,146**	**30,725**

Muslim population in Garo Hills

The population of Garo Hills as a whole is consisted of four distinct religious groups – Adherents of Garo indigenous religion, Christians, Hindus and Muslims. In term of their numerical strength, Muslims were in the fourth position in 1971. This is obvious from Table 10.[4]

The population of Garo Hills rose from 1,21,570 in 1871 to 1,38,274 in 1901. Of the population of 1901, about 82 per cent were adherents to the indigenous religion, 10 per cent were Hindus and 6 per cent were Muslims.[5] In 1981 the total population of West Garo Hills was 3,69,877. Out of this 33,337 were Muslims and their percentage to the total population of the district was 9.01.

Table 10: Religion-wise population of Garo Hills (1961—1971)

Religion	1961		1971	
	Population	%	Population	%
Garo indigenous religion or Songsarek	1,42,274	46.3	1,39,148	34.22
Christianity	87,311	28.42	1,65,715	40.75
Hinduism	51,876	16.88	78,061	19.19
Islam	17,163	5.59	21,929	5.39
Others	1,604	2.80	1,762	0.46

In 1971 the Muslim population of Tura, the district headquarter of West Garo Hills was only 464 in number. Out of this, 319 persons were males and 145 were females.[6]

Muslim population in Khasi Hills

In Khasi Hills majority of the Muslims live in the capital town of Shillong. The Muslim population of the town was

646 in 1901. It increased to 5,154 in1961 and the percentage of the Muslims to the total population of Shillong was 5.03 against that of the Hindus (56.79) and the Christians (25.89). Table 11[7] shows the trend of the Muslim population growth along with that of other religious communities.

It is obvious from the table that the growth of the Muslim population in the state capital of Shillong is slower than that of the Hindus and the Christians. Though the Muslims of Bengal and Assam had long business contact with the hill tribes, they did not migrate to the hills in large number. "During the British period and immediately after independence a large majority of the Hindus migrated to Shillong for trade and employment....out of them the Bengalis, particularly from Bangladesh, form the majority. The Muslim population did not grow as rapidly as the Hindus and Christians."[8] While the Christian population increased rapidly, the growth of the Muslim population remained very slow. This is due to lack of missionary zeal among the Muslims to spread the message of Islam among the local tribes.

Table 11: Religion wise population of Shillong town group

Religion	**1901**	**1911**	**1921**	**1931**	**1941**	**1951**	**1961**
Hindus	3633	5446	6916	13739	20269	34733	58157
Muslims	646	847	991	1423	3026	2418	5154
Christians	879	2162	3542	5171	903	11244	26500
Sikhs	9	53	79	223	511	659	1211
Buddhists	36	51	41	84	217	314	643
Jains	3	4	2	2	—	46	103
Animist tribals	3099	5029	5606	5885	13257	9082	10771
Others	59	—	126	9	9	25	59
Total	**9621**	**13639**	**17203**	**26536**	**38192**	**58512**	**102398**

In the medieval and the British period, only a small number of Muslims came to Meghalaya. The geography and the nature of terrain of hills were not favourable for the movement of people from the plains to the hills. Moreover the hills were steamy, malarious and extremely unhealthy. These factors are responsible for the presence of small percentage of the Muslim population in the total population of the state.

Muslim tribal

Tribal society is matrilineal. A number of Muslims had married tribal women after converting them to Islam. The children born out of these marriages become known as the tribal Muslims. They have been given the title of their mothers following the tribal tradition so that they are not deprived from their right to inherit their ancestoral property and to purchase and own land and house by their own earning in their future life. However, it may be pointed out that in tribal society of Meghalaya, only female can inherit the ancestoral property. The males cannot do so. But they can only own property purchased by their own earning under the Self-Acquired Property Act of the state. However, the Muslim tribal population is very small. Their number is not shown separately in the census report.

It may also be mentioned that some Muslim men having married to tribal women have completely assimilated in the local tribes by adopting their religion, language, culture and tradition for the sake of their women, property and other privileges. They have retained nothing to be called themselves Muslim except their names signifying only that once they were also followers of Islam.

The Muslim tribal women follow their own traditional dress code. They generally do not use headscarf. While offering salat (Muslim prayer) only, they cover their head. The ornaments they commonly use are finger ring, bangles, necklace and earrins.

Divorce and polygamy

The divorce and the polygamy are rare among the Muslims of Meghalaya. As per 1971 census, the percentage of divorce among the Khasi-Pnars of Khasi-Jaintia Hills and the Garos of Tura town was 7.8 and 1.1 percent respectively.[9] Polygamy is frequent and common among the members of all major hill tribes of the state. As per 1961 census report, in India the incidence of polygamous marriage is the highest among the tribals and the lowest among the Muslims (Table 12).

Table 12: Polygamous marriage

Community	*Number of polygamous marriage in percentage*
Tribals	15.25
Buddhists	7.97
Jains	6.72
Hindus	5.8
Muslims	5.7

Muslim literacy

According to 2001 census, the literacy rate of Meghalaya is 63.31 per cent (See Table 13). It is 66.14 percent for males and 60.41 per cent for females. It is for the Muslims, particularly for their women, would be far less than the rate of the whole state. Statistics on the Muslim literacy are not separately available. It is observed that reading habit among the educated Muslims of the state is very poor. Consequently, they do not possess adequate information, knowledge and skill required for proper development of their socio-economic and spiritual life.

Table 13: Literacy of the state (In percentage)

Year	*Male*	*Female*	*Total*
1981	47.75	38.30	42.05
1991	53.12	44.85	49.01
2001	66.14	60.41	63.31

Conclusion

Out of the state's total population of 23,06,069 the Muslims are only 83,487 in number. The statistics relating to their socio-economic condition are not separately available. As a result it has been difficult for intellectuals and researchers to throw sufficient light on their educational, employment, health and economic status as well as on their demographic characteristics. However, this difficulty can be overcome, if Muslim leaders and intellectuals like teachers, lawyers etc. come forward to collect data concerning to their population of their respective areas for the purpose of studying and highlighting their own socio-economic situation for the use of planners and administrators.

ENDNOTES

1. Rahman Mohammad Hasibor. Muslims in Meghalaya. Muslim & Arab Perspective. Vol. 3 Issues1—6 (1996). Pharos Media & Publishing Pvt. Ltd., Abul Fazl Enclave, Jamia Nagar. New Delhi – 110025, P. 150.

2. Pocket Statistical Handbook 2000, Government of Meghalaya, Directorate of Economics & Statistics, Shillong, P. 14.

3. Meghalaya District Gazetteer: Garo Hills, 1996, Edited by I. M. Simon, Government of Meghalaya, Arts & Culture Department, Meghalaya, Shillong, PP. 30 – 31.

4. Ibid, P.34.

5. BCA, EAG, HFH & CGHA, Gazetteer of Bengal and North-East India, 2001, Mittal Publication, A- 110, Mohan Garden, New Delhi—110053, P. 503.

6. Census of India, 1971,Series—13, Meghalaya, P. 155.

7. Mathur P. R. G., The Khasi of meghalaya, 1979, Cosmo Publications, New Delhi, P. 9.

8. Ibid.

9. Meghalaya District Gazetteer: Garo Hills, 1996, P. 38.

CHAPTER IV

Peaceful contact and co-existence

People of different socio-economic groups come into contact with each other for the purpose of satisfying their needs of different goods and services. For such contact physical proximity and communication between individuals or groups are necessary. The Muslims have been having contact with Khasi, Jaintia and Garo tribes for over eight hundred years at four levels - commercial, social, cultural and political.

Business contact

The Muslim of Bengal imported cotton, oranges, betel nuts and leaves, stone, lime, timber etc, from the hill tribes and exported to them kerosene, fish, cotton and silk clothes, rice, salt and other articles of daily needs. This trade link opened the door of a new relationship between the plain people and the hill tribes in other fields of mutual interests. Places like Cherrapunji, Shella and Nongstoin in Khasi Hills, Dawki, Muktapur, Jaintiapur etc. in Jaintia Hills and Mahendraganj, Singimari, Garobada, Pepulbari, etc, in Garo Hills were, in course of time, developed into important trade centres. During the Mughal period Shella became an important business centre and attracted a large number of foreign traders who came from as far as the Middle-East and Persia.[1]

The hill people, particularly the Khasi-Pnars, were keen traders. As the trade relationship between the hills and the plains grew, the hill traders visited the plain region of Bengal as far as Dhaka and Calcutta for commercial purposes. The Muslim traders also visited the different places in the hills. They used to bring essential goods and articles with them from Bengal and sell them to hill people at their local markets. Fasad Khan, who governed Sylhet at the end of the seventeenth century, constructed numerous roads and bridges[2]. With the development of communication in Sylhet the trade between the hills and the plains increased further.

The Khasi chiefs had numerous villages called *duars* in their possession in Kamrup.[3] The Muslims had settled in the Brahmaputra valley in the beginning of the thirteenth century. In1227 Giusuddin ascended the Brahmaputra as far as Sadiya[4]. In 1228 Nasiruddin, eldest son of Altutmish and ruler of Bengal, conquered Kamrup. In 1257 Ikhtiyaruddin Uzbak Tughril Khan, the Turkish governor of Bengal, occupied Kamrup Nagar (North Guwahati) and erected a mosque there.[5] In 1498 Allauddin Hussain Shah[6], governor of Bengal (1493—1513), sent an expedition to Kamata Kingdom that included Kamrup, Goalpara, Dhubri, Kokrajhar, Nalbari, Barpeta and some portions of North Bengal and Mymensing at the persuation of Brahman Councillor of Kamatapur under the leadership of his son-in-law, Dulal Gazi. Dulal Gazi conquered Kamata kingdom upto Hajo and handed over the reign of the new country to Danial, son of Allauddin Hussain Shah. Danial established his capital at Hajo and ruled Kamata for about 17 years till his assassination in 1515 by the rising Bhuyans. He constructed a madrasah at Manda in 1502 and Giasuddin Aulyia, who came to Hajo in 14th century with Dulal Gazi, erected a mosque al-Hajo for the use of the local converts of Islam and preached the message of Islam among the local people from there. Consequently, a large number of natives of Assam embraced Islam impressed by its simplicity and humanism. Like the Muslims of Bengal, Muslim and non-Muslim traders of Kamrup, Nowgong and Goalpara had trade relation with the Khasi and the Garo tribes. This is obvious from the fact that while Jaintia king seized an Ahom trader in 1647, Ahom king Jayadhvaj Singh retaliated by arresting a number of Jaintia traders at Sonapur[7]. Iron and iron manufacturers of the Khasi-Jaintia hills had a big market in medieval Assam[8].

The Muslims of Bengal and Assam alike knew the Khasi and Garo people and their inhabited regions. Shihabuddin Talis who accompanied Mir Jumlah to Assam during 1661—1663 left an account of the expedition of Mir Jumlah and the people of Assam. In his account he mentioned Khasi Hills and Garo hills as the southern border of Assam.[9]

The Garos once occupied a large part of the Brahmaputra valley, but the early Hindu invaders of Bengal drove them into the present hill region from the plains. They were in intermittent conflict with the Hindu zamindars as they levied exorbitant tax on them[10]. However, it appears that their relation with the Muslims was more or less peaceful.

Social contact

The Muslims and the hill tribes had been living side by side for centuries in the plain region at the foot of the hills. They came to know each other and developed mutual trust among them because of their business contacts and deals. The Muslims who married tribal women used to attend the social and family functions of the kinsfolk of their wives as a gesture of goodwill and co-operation. The tribal people also visited the houses of their Muslim friends on the occasion of festivals and marriage. However, main meeting points of the plain and hill people were markets and religious fairs. In course of time, the Muslim settlement spread, though in small numbers, to all major towns and urban areas of the hilly region.

There has been no distinction between a tribal Muslim and a non-tribal Muslim in their religious and social life. They have been living as neighbours to one another and maintaining close social tie over the years. They offer their *Salah** in the same mosque, in the same language (Arabic) and in the same manner. After their death they are buried in the same graveyard. They observe their religious festivals in the same spirit of brotherhood, unity and equality. They have overcome the barrier of communication through the use of English, Urdu and Hindi languages.

Cultural contact

The Muslims, who married tribal women and settled in the hills, generally lived in their wives' houses, learnt the languages of their pouses and adopted some local customs particularly in the matter of inheritance and ownership of landed property as they can not own any property in their names. According to the tribal law of inheritance and ownership, ownership of all their earnings and properties purchased by them automatically passes on to their wives. After the death of their wives, the ownership of property passes on to their youngest daughter. However, the Muslim Khasi parents divide their property among their daughters equally. Male members of the family cannot inherit any property. But they can purchase property by their own earnings and own it. Children born of these marriages often learnt how to recite the Holy Qur'an and offer *Salah*. They also learnt the languages of their parents. This has brought cultural fusion and development of the tribal languages.

In the tribal societies of Meghalaya, women enjoy absolute right to inherit, own and acquire all movable and immovable properties and bear greater responsibility on their shoulder in looking after the affairs of their family. Whatever male member of the family earns before his marriage goes to his mother and after marriage to his wife. In case of divorce, a man is required to go out of his wife's house empty handed leaving behind everything he has earned till seperation his wife. Fate of his marriage tie depends on the sweet will of his wife. Socio- economic position of the tribal man is very pitiable. Christianity could not solve the problems of the tribal family life. Rather it has made the tribal life more miserable than before by making the divorce not permissible. In Islam both man and woman have equal right to inherit, acquire and own all kinds of property. They have equal rights and duties to each other. No one can infringe them. There is enormous scope in Islam for tribal men and women for living with honour and dignity to the best of their satisfaction. There is no other code of life as judicious and impartial as Islam in the world providing scope for development of harmonious and sound family life.

In Islam a wife is, like in the tribal society, entitled to maintain her own identity separate from that of her husband. Marriage does not merge her personality into the personality of her husband. Nor does it confer upon her husband any right over her wealth and income. Nor does it confer upon her any right over the property of her husband. In Muslim marriage a groom is required to give the bride *Mehr,* a sum of money fixed through consultation between the parties in marriage, ornaments, dress, a pair of shoe, cosmetics etc. according to his ability as a mark of love and respect. After the marriage a husband is solely held responsible for the maintenance and protection of his wife and children. In return a wife is required to show her gratitude to her husband. But she retains her full right to express her view on any matter of her familial and social life. Neither the husband nor the wife can whimsically or at will divorce the other. In case of divorce, the wife has the right to take her *Mehr*, all properties acquired by her own earnings and all properties obtained as gifts from her relatives with her. No one in the family can deprive her of her rights.

The Muslims believe in one and only God called Allah. They worship none besides Him. Their God is above all relations, Eternal, Unseen, Beneficent, Merciful, All-Powerful, All-Wise, All-Knower, All-Seer and beyond the perception of all human beings.[11] The Khasis also, like the Muslims, believe in one God Who is unseen and formless. Maham Singh, an eminent Khasi intellectual, has said that the Khasi people believe "in one God whom they only pray but do not offer any sacrifices. In the beginning of the prayer they use the word... 'Oh God, Omnipresent, Lord, Creator, who is within us and is the one and only one....' To the Khasis God is neither faminine nor masculine. He is a formless being, all-powerful. It is sin to worship idols; none can symbolize God for since the beginning of time none has seen Him." [12]

The Muslims are, like the tribal people, friendly, liberal and hospitable. They do not have social evils like, the system of caste, dowry and burning of widow alive on the funeral pyre of her deceased husband. Remarriage of widow is permitted in Islam as well in the tribal system.

Though the Muslims had in many ways physical and cultural proximity with the hill tribes for over six hundred years before the advent of the Christians, they could not pave the way for the spread of Islam in the hills because of lack of organized missionary efforts among them. Islam was found its way into the hills through only mix marriages. Very few Muslim saints like Shah Kamal [13] visited the hilly region for preaching Islam because of difficult terrain and hostile climate. Their visit was limited to the foot of the hills only.

The tribal people of Meghalaya came into contact with the Christianity in 19th century. The Christian missionaries introduced the New Testament among the tribal people in

1924 and then established schools, dispensaries and churches in the hills.[14] They developed tribal languages by bringing out literatures in Roman script. Thus they won over the hill people and got them converted into the fold of Christianity. Now over 64 per cent of the tribal population of the state is the followers of Christianity.

Political contact

It appears that the Khasis and the Jaintias had good relationship with the Muslim rulers of Bengal and Delhi. "Prof. G. G. Swell's unearthing of 14 silver plated coins from a pond in Jowai in Jaintia Hill shows that the Khasi had maintained some sort of trade (and political) relationship with the Mughal emperors of Delhi through their viceroy stationed at Murshidabad."[15] Muslim rulers of Bengal never sent any expedition to conquer the Jaintia kingdom that extended to the Gangetic plain of Bengal. Muslim conquest was limited to Sylhet Proper. It appears that the Khasis and the Jaintias migrated to the plains on the south from their hills on the north after the Muslim conquest of Sylhet in 1303. The Jaintia Kingdom was extended to Jaintiapur in 1500[16]. During the reign of Akbar (1556—1605) Sylhet was incorporated to the Mughal Empire and Lour kingdom was brought under its supremacy. During the reign of Aurangzeb (1658—1707) the king of Lour came into the fold of Islam along with his subjects. The Mughal authorities of Sylhet encouraged the Khasis to migrate to the plains for clearing jungles and bringing land under cultivation.[17] They also inducted the hill chiefs in the plains and permitted them to get land cultivated by the Bengali peasants.[18] Following this a large number of Khasis and Jaintias settled in Sylhet and Lour. This shows that the over all relationship between the Muslims of Bengal and the hill tribes was cordial and peaceful.

During the British period the relation of the Muslims with the hill tribes in the hill region was further enhanced particularly in the political arena. Sheikh Muhammad Amjad Ali was appointed as the legal adviser of the Syiem of Mylliem. He was also elected as the Commissioner of Shillong Municipal Board in 1929 and then to the Assam Legislative Council from Shillong. In 1937 S. M. Saadullah became the Premier of Assam and included a tribal leader as minister in his cabinet. Saleh Muhammad Akbar Hydari was the Governor of Assam from May, 1947 to December, 1948. Both Saadullah and Akbar Hydari enjoyed full confidence of the tribal people because of their sincerity and positive out look to the tribal affairs. Even after independence of India, the Muslim leaders of the hills and the plains of Assam alike had maintained their political relationship with all major communities and political parties of the hill districts. After creation of Meghalaya, Muhammad Sayeedullah Nongrum, a Khasi political leader of Shillong, was elected to the Meghalaya State Legislative Assembly in 1983 and 2003 from Rajabala Reserved Assembly constituency that is located in West Garo Hills district. This speaks volume of the relationship of the Muslims and the hill tribes in the hill state.

Conclusion

Since the beginning of the 13th century the Muslims and the hill tribes have been maintaining co-operation in the field of Politics, commerce and agriculture for their mutual benefit. This has resulted in cross-fertilization of their professional ideas and skill as well as development of mutual understanding of their needs of good and services. Thus they have realized the importance of their co-existence and co-operation in the plains and the hills of the state. The conflict and contradiction that had occurred at some points of times on the way of their socio-political relationship could not deter them from living peacefully as the neighbour of eachother.

ENDNOTES

1. Warjri E, The Shella Wahadadarship: The Roots of Polity Formation in the War area of East Khasi Hills District, Proceedings of North-East India History Association, Seventh Session, Pasighat, 1986, edited and published by J. B. Bhattacharjee on behalf of North-East India History Association, Department of History, North-Eastern Hill University, Shillong, P. 117

2. Gait Edward, A History of Assam, 1997, LBS Publications,Guwahati, Assam, P. 263

3. Gurdon P. R. T., The Khasi, P. XVIII.

4. Tabaqat-I-Nasiri, Reverty's translation, Vol. I, P. 594.

5. Ibid, P. 263.

6. Gait Edward, Op. Cit., PP. 41- 42.

7. Ibid, P 119.

8. Guha A., Medievel Norht East India (1200—1750), Occasional paper No. 19, Centre for Studies in Social Sciences, Calcutta, P. 25, quoted in Dutta Sushil Chandra, The North East and Mughals (1661—1714), 1984, D. K. publications, 29 / 9, Nangia Park, Shakti Nagar, Delhi – 110007, P. 222.

9. Gait Edward, Op. Cit., P. 133.

10. BCA, EAG, HFH & CGHA, The Gazetteer of Bengal and North-East India, 2001, Mittal Publications, New Delhi—110059, P.502.

11. The Muslim Prayers

12. For details, see the following verses of the Holy Qur'an

Surah 1: Ayah 1— 4

Surah 2: Ayah 163

Surah 20: Ayah 114

Surah 42: Ayah 11

Surah 56: Ayah 105

Surah59: Ayah 23 & 24

Surah 89: Ayah 14

Surah112:Ayah 1—4

13. Mathur P.R.G., The Khasi of Meghalaya, 1979, Cosmo Publications, New Delhi, P. 24.

14. Meghalaya District Gazetteer: Garo Hills Districts, 1996, edited by Simon I. M., Government of Meghalaya, Arts and Culture Department, Shillong, PP.235—236.

15. Mathur P. R. G. Op. Cit., PP. 13—21.

16. Ibid, P. 43.

17. Gait Edward, Op. Cit., 1984, L.B.S. Publications, Guwahati, Assam, P. 261.

18. Firminger A., Sylhet District Records Vol. III

19. Gurdon P.R.T., OP. Cit., PP.189—90.

CHAPTER V

Muslims in the Development of Meghalaya

The process of economic development of the hill region of today's Meghalaya was actually started with the advent of the Muslim traders of Bengal into the hills. Before the coming of the Muslims, the region was full of dense forests. Rainfall was very heavy. Economy was completely agrarian and under developed. The three tribal groups—the Khasi, the Jaintia and the Garo—lived in three distinct regions—Khasi Hills, Jaintia Hills and Garo Hills—in an isolated manner. Their standard of living was very low. They wore scanty cloth. Their houses were cachcha and temporary. Road communication in the hills was very difficult and perilous.

Trade and commerce

It is already known that the Muslim businessmen from Assam and Bengal frequented the different parts of the hilly region. Besides selling their goods, they bought different products of the Hill men and took them to their homeland for sale. This practice of the traders from the plains increased economic activities in the hill and encouraged many tribal people to take up business as their profession. When the British annexed the Garo Hills and the Khasi-Jaintia Hills to their empire, their officials found a large number of tribal people, particularly among the Khasis and the Jaintias, earning their livelihood by trade and recorded this thus: "The hill men are keen traders, and a considerable proportion of the people earn their living by travelling from one market to another."[1]

In 1866 when the headquarter of the Khasi-Jaintia Hills was shifted from Cerrapunji to Shillong, the British officials brought a Muslim businessman named Gulam Hydar with them from there to help them to settle in their new establishment. Gulam Hydar had come from Hoogly district of West Bengal and settled in Cherrapunji. In that year itself, he opened a departmental store named 'Gulam Hydar & Sons' in the present police Bazar of Shillong town where every thing except wine and cigerate was available. He was the first businessman to settle down in Shillong. Later on, Jamatullah, Abdul Gafoor and N.K. Bhattacharya had also set up their own respective departmental store in Shillong.[2] It appears that Gulam Hydar had come to Cherrapunji after the political agent of the East India Company made Cherrapunji his new administrative headquarter in 1834.

Agriculture

Generally soil in the hilly region contains pebbles and is less fertile and red in colour. It is in the plain region bordering Assam and Bangladesh, particularly in Garo Hills, dark in colour and more fertile than that of the Hills. The hill tribes practise Jhum or shifting cultivation on the slopes of the hills. The instruments used for the purpose of cultivation of land are mainly hoe or digging stick, spade and dao. The chief produces are rice maize, potato, tapioca, millet, pulses, rape, mustard, ginger, black pepper, etc. Besides these, betel nut, betel leaf, orange, pineapple, banana, turmeric, chilly, cotton etc. are produced in the hills. The Muslim farmers in the plain areas use plough and spade for cultivating their land. They produce paddy, jute, wheat, pulses and different kinds of vegetables. Thus they have been giving much needed impetus to the state's economy.

In 1830 David Scott introduced potato cultivation in the Khasi Hills.[3] The Muslim farmers introduced cultivation of jute, wheat, barley, potato and other food and cash crops in Assam and in the plain portions of the Jaintia kingdom and the Garo Hills long before the coming of the British in the North-East India. In 1924 Syed Muhammad Saadullah (1885 -1955) became minister of the province of Assam for Agriculture and Education. During the tenure of his ministership the process of actual development of agriculture in terms of productivity and method of cultivation was started. The land area under cultivation had also begun to increase. After becoming premier of Assam, Saadullah adopted the government of India's grow more food scheme to avert the occurrence of Bengal type famine in Assam. The Garos borrowed cows from Muslim farmers and hired Muslim agricultural labours from the plains of Bengal and Assam for cultivating their lands lying in the level valleys by plough in some places of Garo. Hills bordering Assam.[4] In 1998-1999 the total cropped area of the state was increased to 2,62,830 hectres out of the state's total geographical area of 22, 48, 900 hectres.[5]

Industry

The Khasis made heavy jewellery and manufactured pottery, iron hoes and daos. The Jaintias wove clothes and jackets from thread spun from silkworm and cotton. They also made bamboo mats and cane baskets and sieves.[6] In Garo Hills women wove a kind of course cotton cloth in blue dye with red stripes for them and their men. Bamboo baskets and mats were also made for sale. Rude pottery was made in certain villages and all metal utensils they used were imported.[7] With the appearance of Muslim and Hindu artisans and technicians and later on, Christian missionaries in the hilly region, the process of modernization of the primitive economy was started. The design and quality of the products of the old industries was improved. New business enterprises like jewellery, automobile workshop, printing press, tailoring, bakery, blacksmithy, quilt making, saloon, laundry etc. were established. Gulam Hydar's departmental store introduced concept of banking for the first time in Shillong.[8] Haji Qusimuddin set up printing press, milk dairy and soda water factory in the capital town. A good number of Muslims have been having their own business establishments till to this day in Meghalaya.

The Mughal authorities of Bengal took the lime stone quarries of Lour (Nongstoin-Langrin) hills on lease and employed Bengali labours to work there.[9] They took active interest in lime stone quarries and gradually assumed the monopoly of the lime trade.[10] While the Mughals had the control of the lime stones of the Lour Hills, the private traders of Bengal used to take on lease limestone quarries of other parts of the Khasi-Jaintia hills.[11] From this it is understandable that the Muslims and the Hindus played an important role in the development of lime stone quarries and lime trade in the hills and the plains alike.

Road and building

Before the occupation of the Khasi-Jaintia hills and the Garo hills by the British, the hilly region was very backward in road communication. In the 19th century there was only 97 miles long metalled cart-road running from Cherrapunji to Guwahati via Shillong. A Tanga and bullock-cart service was available between Cherrapunji and Guwahati. In 1903-1904 altogether 356 miles of bridle path were there in the Khasi-Jaintia hills. In the same year there were altogether 73 miles cart-road and 126 miles bridle path in the Garo hills.[12] In 1998-1999 there were 3889 kms surfaced and 2982 kms unsurfaced roads in Meghalaya.[13]

It appears that since the middle part of the 19th century the Muslim engineer, architect, builder, carpenter, mason and other skill and semi-skill labourers have been playing an important role in the construction and development of roads, bridges and buildings in the hill state of Meghalaya. In 1903 Qusimuddin, son of Gulam Hydar, introduced the first passenger bus services between Shillong and Guwahati. He also constructed the mosque located at Police Bazar in Shillong and the church of England situated between State Central Library and Government Printing Press. He was honoured with title of 'Khan Bahadur' by the then British government in recognition of his public services.[14] Following the introduction of the bus services, motor workshops like Khan Motors, Sharif Motors, Negi Motors etc. were set up in the Police Bazar.[15] Moula Buksh, son of Qusimuddin Khan Bahadur, was a reputed builder of Shillong. "He constructed a number of buildings in Police Bazar, Polo Ground and other localities"[16].

Education

Before the advent of the Christian missionaries, the level of education among the people living in the hilly region of present day Meghalaya was at the bottom. There was hardly any educational institution in the hills. A very few people went to Bengal for study. The Christian missionaries established the first primary school at Cherrapunji in Khasi Hills in 1833,[17] at Jowai in Jaintia hills in 1854[18] and at Tura in Garo hills in 1879[19]. In 1901 percentage of literate people in Khasi-Jaintia hills and Garo hills was 5.7 and 0.8 respectively[20]. The Muslims established their first primary school called Islamia Madrasah at Police Bazar in Shillong in 1920. Islamia Madrasah was raised to the status of M.E. school in 1931-32. Now it is upgraded to higher secondary school. Himayat-ul-Islam M.E. School was established in 1953 at Garikhana in Shillong. A Muslim Girls Lower Primary School was also established at Laban.

Mr. Mondon Bareh, Deputy Inspector of schools of Khasi and Jaintia Hills had shown the progress of Muslim education in Chapter X of his review on the progress of education in Khasi and Jaintia Hills from 1926-27 to 1931-32 as in Table 14.[21]

Table 14: Figures of enrolment of Muslim students

Class of institutions	No. of Muslim students		Percentage of increase or decrease
	1926-27	1931-32	
High schools	12	28	133.3
M.E. schools	14	111	693.0
Primary schools	49	3	-93.8
Total	75	142	89.3

Noting the decrease in the enrolment of the Muslim students in primary schools, Mr. Mondon Bareh recorded the reason of the decrease in these words in his report: "The decrease in enrolment in primary schools is due to the fact that during the last quinquennium the Islamia Madrasah, which is the only institution for Muhammadans, was raised to the status of an M.E. school."

In West Garo Hills district there are four M.E. Madrasahs under the control of the Board of School Education, Meghalaya as given in the Table 15[22]. Besides Assamese, Bengali and English languages, Arabic and Urdu are taught in these Madrasahs. The total number of students enrolled in the madrasahs was 351 in 1996.

Table 15: M.E. Madrasahs

<table>
<tr><th>Name of Madrasah</th><th>Year of establishment</th><th>No. of pupils</th><th>No. of teachers</th></tr>
<tr><td>Belarchar M.E. Madrasah</td><td>1980-81</td><td rowspan="4">351</td><td rowspan="4">23</td></tr>
<tr><td>Bhaitbari M.E. Madrasah</td><td>1980-81</td></tr>
<tr><td>H & N M.E. Madrasah</td><td>1980-81</td></tr>
<tr><td>Anjuman M.E. Madrasah</td><td>1982</td></tr>
<tr><td>Total</td><td></td><td>351</td><td>23</td></tr>
</table>

The Muslims of Meghalya have established a good number of educational institutions in different places of the state. The Shillong Muslim Union established Umshyrpi College at Laban in April, 1994.[23] Twenty percent seats are kept reserved in the college for the students of the Muslim community. In all these Muslims run educational institutions students from all communities are admitted and taught. Educated youth of these institutions have been serving the state in different capacities.

Health

Before the establishment of dispensaries, the Muslim physicians called Hakim had played an important role in treating diseased persons and promoting health and vitality of the people particularly those who settled in the plain at the foot of the hills. These Hakims treated their patients with medicines made of onion, garlic, honey, mustard oil, fruit, herb, leaf, root and stem of different kinds of trees and plants mentioned in the Holy Qur'an and Prophetic traditions. Some Muslim saints like Shah Jalal and Shah Kamal as well as Imam of mosque helped many sick persons to get free from their health problems by the strength of their spiritual knowledge, power and experience.

Shah Kamal taught his wife how to prepare medicines from herb and shrubs, drive away evil spirit and treat the sick people. His wife became very powerful and served the needy people following the noble example set by her husband.[24]

Conclusion

Since their advent in this hilly region of India the Muslims have been actively engaged in the development of their adopted land hand in hand with the hill people. They have contributed substantially to the growth of new technology, arts, crafts and architecture in the region. But they are lagging behind other communities in their socio-economic life. The state government is required to remove their economic and educational backwardness and enable them to contribute more effectively than what they did before in the developmental programmes of the state.

ENDNOTES

1. BCA, EAG HFH & CGHA, Gazetteer of Bengal and North-East India, 2001, Mittal Publications, A-110, Mohan Garden, New Delhi110059, P. 491.
2. Ray Anirban, Where Shillong means business, The Hindustan Times North-East Live, Saturday, September 6, 2001, P. 3.
3. Allen B.C., Gazetteer of the Khasi & Jaintia Hills, Garo Hills and Lushai Hills, PP. 73-74.
4. Hussain Mohammad Tabarak, 80 years, Village: Kukurmara under Mankachar police station in Dhubri district of Assam, date 25-10-2001.
5. District Level Statistics, 2002, Government of Meghalaya, Directorate of Economics & Statistics, Meghalaya, Shillong, P. 1.
6. BCA, EAG HFH & CGHA, Op.Cit., P. 491.
7. Ibid, P. 509.
8. Ray Anirban, Op. Cit.
9. Bengal Judicial (Cr.) Consultation, Moor to Bayley, 12 May1823, No.39; 5 June, 1823, No.41, Cited in Dutta P. N., Relations of the Khasis and Jaintias with their southern neighbours till the British intervention, paper presented in the First session of North-East India History Association, Shillong, 1980, P. 77.
10. Bengal Revenue Consultation, 24 September, 1790, No. 42, cited in Ray B. Dutta, Khasi Hills and Brahmo Samaj Movement, Paper Presented in the First session of North-East India History Association, Shillong, 1980 and in Dutta Sushil Chandra, The North-East and the Mughals (1661-1714), 1984, D. K. Publications, Nangia Park, Shakti Nagar, Delhi-110007, P. 222.
11. Dutta P.N., Op. Cit.
12. BCA, EAG HFH & CGHA, Op. Cit., PP. 492 & 509.
13. District Level Statistics, 2002, Government of Meghalaya, Directorate of Economics & Statistics, Meghalaya, Shillong, P. 1.
14. Mathur P.R.G., The Khasi of Meghalaya, 1979, Cosmo Publications, New Delhi, P. 43.
15. Ray Anirban, Op. Cit.
16. Mathur P.R.G. Op. Cit., P. 44.
17. Bareh Hamlet, Progress of Education in Meghalaya, 1996, Cosmo Publications for Genesis Publishing Pvt., Ltd., 24-B, Ansari Road, Daya Ganj, New Delhi-110002, P. 151.
18. Meghalaya District Gazetteer (MDG): Jaintia Hills, edited by I. M. Simon, 1996, Government of Meghalaya, Arts and Culture Department, Shillong, P. 181.

19. MDG: Garo Hills. Ibid. P. 185.
20. BCA. EAG. HFH. & CGHA Op. Cit.. PP. 493 & 510.
21. Bareh Hamlet. Op. Cit., PP. 286-287.
22. MDG: Garo Hills. Op.Cit. P. 193.
23. Umshyrpi – The Mirror. Annual Publication. 2002. edited by Asif Ibrahim. Published by Umshyrpi College. Laban. Shillong.
24. MDG: Garo Hills. Op. Cit., P. 236.

CHAPTER VI

Muslim representation in the State Legislative Assembly

Before the creation of Meghalaya on 21st January 1972, the entire area of the state was a part of Assam. Prior to the enactment of the Government of India Act of 1935, the region was not adequately represented in the Assam Legislative Council as it was then backward. Under the Diarchy introduced in 1921 in Assam "the government consisted of two parts, the Reserved and the Transferred. The Reserved half was administered by an Executive Council consisting of two members."[1] A two member Council of Ministers administered the other half of the government. The Muslims had adequate representation in both Executive Council and Council of Ministers.

Executive Council

"The members of the Executive Council were appointed by His Majesty by Warrant under the Royal sign Manual for a term of five years."[2] The Executive Council was always consisted of one Indian and one European. There were altogether four Indian members – three Muslims from the Assam valley and one Hindu from the Surma valley - of the Executive Council from 1921 to 1937 (Table 16).

Table 16: Indian Members of the Executive Council (1921-1937)

Sl	Name	Term of Office
1	Abdul Majid	1921 - 1924
2	Kutbuddin	1924 - 1929
3	Syed Muhammad Saadullah	1929 - 1934
4	P.C. Dutta	1934 – 1937

Council of Ministers

The governor used to appoint members of the Council of Ministers from among the members who possesses the confidence of the state Legislative Council. Both members of the Council of Ministers were always Indians. There were altogether seven members – three Muslims, three Hindus and one Christian - of the Council of Ministers from 1921 to 1937. The Muslim members are listed in Table 17.

Table 17: Muslim Members of Council of Ministers (1921-1937)

Sl	Name	Term of Office
1	Saiyid Abdul Majid (From Surma Valley)	1921 - 1923
2	Syed Muhammad Saadullah (From Assam Valley)	1924 – 1926 & 1926 - 1929
3	Abdul Hamid (From Surma Valley)	1929 – 1937

Assam State Legislative Council

Prior to 1912 Assam did not have its own legislative

council. In 1912 it was reconstituted into a Chief Commissioner's province and the Khasi - Jaintia Hills and the Garo Hills were included in it. It was given Legislative Council of 24 members – 13 members were to be nominative of the Chief Commissioner of the province and 11 elective. Out of the 11 elective seats, the Muslims were allotted two seats – one each from the Surma Valley and the Assam Valley.

Under the Government of India Act, 1919, the number of members of the Legislative Council was increased from 24 to 53 – 41members were to be elective and 13 nominative. Out of the 41 elective seats, the Muslims were given 12 seats – four in Assam Valley and eight in Surma Valley.

The Khasi–Jaintia and the Garo Hills were under represented to the Legislative Council because of lack of leaders among the hill people. In 1923 Sheikh Muhammad Amjad Ali (1868 – 1926), the first poet in the Khasi language, was elected to the Assam Legislative Council from Shillong as a representative of the hill people. He was, perhaps, the first and the last Muslim to be elected to the Legislative Council from Shillong.

Under the Government of India Act of 1935, bicameralism was introduced in 1937. The upper house was called Legislative Council and the lower house the Legislative Assembly. Prior to 1937 there was only one legislative body in Assam. The Legislative Council had 22 seats out of which four seats were to be filled up by nomination and the rest by election. Out of the 18 elective seats six seats were allotted to Muslims, two seats to Europeans and the rest were general seats.

Presiding Officer of Legislative Council

The Presiding Officer of the Legislative Council was called President during 1912–1947. There were three Muslim presiding officers in the Legislative council during the said period.

Moulana Abdul Hamid was the first Muslim Presiding Officer and Mrs. Zubida Ataur Rahman the first lady presiding officer of the Assam Legislative Council (Table 18).

Table 18: Muslim Presiding Officers (1912 – 1946)

Name	Term of office
Moulana Abdul Hamid	1925 – 1927 & 1927 – 1929
Faiznur Ali	1929 – 1937 -
Mrs. Zubida Ataur Rahman	1943 – 1945

The Muslim Deputy presiding officers of the legislative Council were Muhabuddin Ahmed (1921–1922), Muhammad Bakhat Mazumdar (1922 -) and Mrs. Zubida Ataur Rahman (1937 – 1943). Mrs. Rahman is the first Muslim lady in the northeastern region of India to hold the post of Deputy Speaker of the Assam Legislative Council.

In 1937 Muhammad Amiruddin was elected as the Deputy Speaker of the Assam Legislative Assembly and continued to hold the office till1946. On March 14, 1946 Mrs. Bonily Khongmen was elected, unopposed, as the Deputy Speaker of the Assembly. She is the first tribal lady to hold this office in the North-East India.

Assam Legislative Assembly

Under the Government of India Act, 1935, the strength of the Assam legislative Assembly was 108 seats out of which two seats were allotted to Garo Hills, two seats to Khasi Hills and one seat to Jaintia Hills. All the 108 seats were elective.

The election to the Assam Legislative Assembly was held in 1937. The verdict was fractured one. No political party could win absolute majority in the state legislature. Party wise position of the elected members of the Assembly was as given in Table 19.[3]

Table 19: Party wise Number of elected members of Assam Legislative Assembly (1937)

Name of Party	Number of elected members
Congress	32
Assam Valley United Peoples Party	8
Progressive Party	12
European Group	13
Independent Party	4
Constitutionalist Party	4
Assam Valley Muslim Party	13
Surma Valley Muslim Party	17
Muslim League	4
Independents	1
Total	**108**

The Congress won highest number of seats that is 32. But the number was not enough for forming the government of its own. "Further, (the Congress) had not decided whether to accept office... It is true that the A.P.C.C. was anxious to accept office but the Working committee had not decided to accept office. The Mahatma laid down certain conditions as regards the exercise of special powers by the Governor. The Governor General did not accept them."[4]

The Muslim League won only four seats from the Surma Valley. "In the Brahmaputra Valley the league had no existence at the time of election and leading Muslims of the valley like Md. Sadullah, Fakruddin Ali Ahmed, Sayidur Rahman and Keramat Ali were elected as independents"[5]

In 1937 total number of Muslim members elected to the Assam Legislative Assembly was 44. But they were divided among the different political parties as in Table 20.[6]

Table 20: Muslim elected member in Assam Legislative Assembly (1937)

Name of party	Number of elected Muslims members
Assam Valley Muslim Party	15
Muslim League	9
Independent Muslims	14
Muslim Praja Party	1
Surma Valley Muslim Party	5
Total	**44**

Formation of ministry

After considering the whole situation governor Michael

Keane came to the conclusion that a leader who would be able enjoy confidence of the majority members of the house should be invited to form the government. He found Syed Muhammad Saadullah to be such a leader and invited him to form the government. But, in the mean time, Robert Reid took over the office of the governor of the province. He also, like his predecessor, invited Saadullah to help him in forming a stable government in the state and asked him to meet him in Shillong. On March 15, 1937, Saadullah came over to Shillong from Calcutta where he was practicing Law at High Court and visited the governor. The governor gave him the green signal for starting the process for forming the government. After making necessary consultation and negotiation with all political parties who are willing to form government under his leadership, Saadullah formed a four member Council of Ministers headed by him. The ministry took oath of office on April 1, 1937. The composition of the first Saadullah ministry was as follows:

1. Syed Muhammad Saadullah (Premier)
2. Muhammad Waheed
3. Ali Hydar Khan
4. J.J.M. Nichols Roy

After the formation of the Saadullah ministry, the Congress made an alliance with the Muslim League to topple the new ministry. Saadullah met the challenge made by the Congress astutely by joining the Muslim League and agreeing to accommodate two members of the Muslim League in his cabinet. Then he expanded and reconstituted his ministry on February 5, 1938. He included two Muslim League members and two Hindus in his ministry and dropped his two colleagues. The tribal member of his cabinet remained the same. The second Saadullah ministry was thus consisted of the following members:

1. Syed Muhammad Saadullah (Premier)
2. J.J.M. Nichols Roy
3. Rohini Kumar Choudhury
4. Munowwar Ali
5. Abdul Matin Choudhury
6. Akshaya Kumar Das

In the aftermath of the Congress-Muslim League alliance, the Muslim League derived maximum political benefit. Besides getting its two members included in the Saadullah ministry and its one candidate elected as Deputy Speaker, it had Premier Saadullah as its member and sowed its seed in the Brahmaputra Valley. The Congress got its candidate elected as Speaker of the state Legislative Assembly only.

But Saadullah's problem was not over. The two dropped ministers went against him and the Congress extended its support to them. Soon some tribal leaders also shifted their loyalties. Akshaya Kumar Das, a minister of the Saadullah ministry, deserted the Premier without resigning from his position. On September 11, 1938 four no-confidence motions were brought against the Saadulla ministry. It was not difficult for Saadullah to understand that he had already lost the confidence of the house. On September 13, 1938 he submitted his resignation without looking for any clue for buying time for horse-trading and "advised the

Governor to call for Gopinath Bordoloi to form the Government."[7] The house profusely praised him for his straightforward resignation and fragrance of the beauty of his personality spread far and wide. Saadullah lost his ministry but gained popularity and good will of the people of the state immensely.

Formation of Bordoloi Ministry

Gopinath Bordoloi claimed that he had the support of the majority of the members of the state Assembly and the governor asked him to form the ministry. On September 19, 1938 Bordoloi installed a five-member ministry and in October of the same year expanded his ministry by including three Muslim ministers. But he was unable to prove his majority for over two months. At last on December 1, 1938 he was able to prove his majority on the floor of the house. The members of the Bordoloi Ministry were:

1. Gopinath Bordoloi (Premier)
2. Akshaya Kumar Das
3. Ramnath Das
4. Kamini Kumar Das
5. Rupnath Brahma
6. Fakharuddin Ali Ahmed
7. Mahmud Ali
8. Ali Hydar Khan

However, it is to be noted here that Gopinath Bordoloi was neither able to form the government nor prove his support of the majority of the members of the house of his own because of differences among the Congress leaders of the state over the formation of the ministry. " It was Subhas Chandra Bose who helped Bordoloi not only in forming the ministry but also in ironing out difference with the Congressmen in the Surma Valley over the formation of the ministry."[8]

The Second World War was started on September 29, 1939 and Britain was not willing to grant freedom to India. The Congress Working Committee had, therefore, decided not to support the war effort and asked the Congress ministries in the Provinces to resign. Following this, Bordoloi submitted his resignation on November 15, 1939 with reluctance, but "Surprisingly enough recommended to the governor the suspension of the constitution on the ground that no one would be able to form the government."[9] But he was proved wrong. Saadullah was a prominent political leader of Assam and commanded respect from all sections of people because of his honesty, sincerity and experience. "Though his party had a strength of 34 members only in a house of 108, his supporters never numbered less than fifty-two."[10]

The governor was well aware of the position of Saadullah and invited him to form the government. The Congress made tremendous effort to prevent Saadullah from forming the government by projecting J.J.M. Nichols Roy as the leader of the coalition Party but in vain. Saadullah established his ministry and took oath of office on November 17, 1939 along with his ministers as listed below:

Third Saadullah Ministry (1939-1941)

1. Syed Muhammad Saadullah (Premier)
2. Rohini Kumar Choudhury
3. Munowwar Ali
4. Hirendra Chandra Chakravarty
5. Mahendra Nath Saikia
6. Abdul Matin Choudhury
7. Sayidur Rahman
8. Miss. Mavis Dunn
9. Mudabbir Hussain Choudhury
10. Rupnath Brahma

In December 1941 Rohini Kumar Choudhury suddenly resigned from the ministry. As a result Saadullah lost the support of the majority members of the house and resigned on December 9, 1941. The governor accepted Saadullah's resignation on December 25, 1941 and declared his rule in the state. Thus the province of Assam was under the governor's rule from December 25, 1941 to August 24, 1942.

On August 25, the governor rule was withdrawn and Saadullah was invited to form the government once again. On the same day Saadullah formed his fourth ministry with the following ministers:

Fourth Saadullah Ministry (1942-1945)

1. Syed Muhammad Saadullah (Premier)
2. Munowwar Ali
3. Mudabbir Hussain Choudhury

4. Sayidur Rahman
5. Abdul Matin Choudhury
6. Hirendra Chandra Choudhury
7. Miss. Mavis Dunn
8. Mahendra Nath Saikia
9. Rupnath Brahma
10. Naba Kumar Dutta.

This ministry of Saadullah was more or less stable. But gradually it appeared to be instable. "The instability was mainly due to the Congress whose members increased as a result of release from the prison."[11] Saadullah had, therefore, made an agreement to form coalition government with the opposition parties. Gopinath Bordoloi agreed to extend his party's support to the proposed coalition government. Saadullah resigned on March 22, 1945 and installed the new coalition ministry headed by him on March 23 with the following members:

Fifth Saadullah Ministry (1945-1946)

1. Syed Muhammad Saadullah (Premier)
2. Munowwar Ali
3. Abdul Matin Choudhury
4. Sayidur Rahman
5. Mudabbir Hussain Choudhury
6. Rohini Kumar Choudhury
7. Baidya Nath Mukharjee
8. Akshaya Kumar Das
9. Surendranath Buragohain
10. Rupnath Brahma

In 1946, election to the Assam Legislative Assembly was held. The Congress won 57 seats, Muslim League 31 seats and Jamiat-ul-Ulema-e-Hind three seats in the house of 108 seats. On February 10,1946 Saadullah submitted the resignation of his ministry and became the leader of the opposition in the state Legislature. On February 11 a nine member Congress government headed by Gopinath Bordoloi was formed. In the Bordoloi ministry only two Muslim leaders – Abdul Matlib Mazumdar and Abdur Rashid – were included. After the independence of India, Saadullah dissolved the Muslim League and joined the Congress party. "He was personally responsible for bringing about a Muslim-Congress entente in Assam before the election of 1952. Differences over nomination of Muslim candidates led to his resignation from the party. But the Assam Muslims in general continuously supported the Congress till the election of 1978"[12]

Before the independence of India, Muslims played pivotal role in the politics of Assam. Shillong was the center of their politics as it was the capital of the united province of Assam. Their political ideas and activities helped the development of political consciousness among the tribal people of the hilly region of Assam. Muslims living in the hilly region did not feel the need for separate representation in the state Legislature as their interests were looked after by the Muslim representatives of their neighbouring plains.

After the partition of India, the political dominance of the Muslims in Assam politics began to decline. With the transfer of Sylhet the number of Muslim elected representatives in the state Assembly was reduced from

34 to 18. Abdul Hamid Khan, the most powerful and popular peasant leader of Assam, left India in 1950. Before 1952 election the Muslims joined the Indian National Congress en masse. Syed Muhammad Saadullah died in 1955. The number of the Muslim ministers in the Council of Ministers during 1946-1972 is reflected in Table 21.[13]

Table 21: Muslims in Assam Cabinet (1946-1972)

Period	Chief Minister	Number of Ministers	Muslim
01-04-1946 to 06-08-1950	G. N. Bordoloi	7 – 9	1 -2
06-08-1950 to 28-12-1957	B. R. Medhi	9	1
28-12-1957 to 06-11-1970	B. P. Chaliha	10 – 18	2
06-11-1970 to 30-01-1972	M. M. Choudhury	26	4

Under the constitution of India the number of seat in the Assam Legislative Assembly was increased from 108 to 126 in 1967. Out of the 126 seats, the Garo Hills and the Khasi Hills were given four seats each and the Jaintia Hills was allotted one seat. When the Autonomous state of Meghalaya was created, a provisional Legislative Assembly was set up. The Assembly consisted of 41 members. Out of these, 38 members were to be elected indirectly by the members of the Autonomous District Councils and three members were to be nominated. Out of the 38 elective seats, the Garo Hills was given 14, the Khasi Hills 18 and the Jaintia Hills six seats. After Meghalaya was declared full-fledged state in 1972, the number of seats in the new state Legislative Assembly was increased from 41 to 60. All members of the house were to be elected directly by the people of the new state. Out of the 60 seats the Garo Hills was allotted 24, the Khasi Hills 30 and the Jaintia

Hills six seats. The present district wise number of seat is as given in Table 22.

Table 22: District wise number of the state Legislative Assembly seats (as on 2003)

District	Number of Assembly seats
West Garo Hills	15
East Garo Hills	7
South Garo Hills	2
West Khasi Hills	8
East Khasi Hills	17
Ri Bhoi	4
Jaintia Hills	7
Total	**60**

Muslim Legislators in the Hills (1972 – 2003)

Out of the 60 Legislative Assembly Constituencies (LAC), non-tribal candidates could contest in only seven constituencies though all seats were initially kept open for all communities of the state. The Muslim candidates could contest in only three LACs – Mahendraganj, Rajabala and Phulbari. In 1993, 55 LACs were declared reserved for the hill tribes as the Bodo, the Rava, the Hajong and the Koch communities were granted Schedule Tribe status. Now only five Legislative Assembly seats –Laban, Pynthorumkhrah, Mawprem, Mahendraganj and Phulbari – are left unreserved. The Muslim candidates can now contest in only two seats - Mahendraganj and Phulbari L. A. constituencies. Till 1998, a total of 10 non-tribal candidates are elected from Phulbari, and Mahendraganj LACs. Of these five were Muslims and the rest were non-Muslims. Abdus Saleh was elected from Mahendraganj

LAC in 1998 at the age of 26 years and set the record of being the youngest MLA in India.

Prior to and after the reservation of Rajabala LAC as many as four non-Garo candidates were elected from there. Out of these three were Muslims and one was Hindu. In 1993 Sayeedullah Nongrum, a tribal Muslim of Shillong, was elected from the reserve constituency. In 1998 a Hindu scheduled caste candidate won the seat. In 2003 Mr. Nongrum was elected from the constituency for the second time. Table 23 gives a picture of the Muslim members of Meghalaya Legislative Assembly.

Table 23: Constituency-wise elected Muslim members of Meghalaya Legislative Assembly (1972 –1998)

	Elected from	
Mahendraganj LAC	***Phulbari LAC***	***Rajabala LAC***
Shams ul Haque (1972 -78)	A. Jaman (1970-1972) (1970 -1978)	Mazibur Rahman (1978–1983)
Abdus Saleh (1998-2003)	Manirul Islam Sarkar (1993-1998 & 2003 -)	Kurshidur Rahman Khan (1983-188)
	Abu Taher Mondal (1998 – 2003)	Sayeedullah Nongrum (1993-1998) & (2003 -)

After the creation of Meghalaya as many as eight Muslim candidates were elected to the Meghalaya Legislative Assembly. During the last thirty-two years, except four, no Muslim member was sworn in as minister. In 2000, Abu Taher Mondal was Included in the E.K. Mawlong ministry as a minister of state for Public Works Department for a short period. Prior to this he was included in the B.B. Lyngdoh ministry and became the first non-tribal minister of Meghalaya. In 2001 Abdus Saleh was included in the Mawlong ministry as a minister of state and given the independent charge of Science and Technology. After the fall of Mawlong ministry, Dr, F.A. Khonglam formed 37member ministry headed by him on December 8, 2001. Abdus Saleh was again included in the Khonglam ministry as a minister of state and given the portfolio of Weights and Measures. In 2003 Manirul Islam Sarkar is included as cabinet minister in the D. D. Lapang Ministry and given the portfolio of Transport and Sayeedullah Nongrum as the cabinet minister with the portfolio of Labour, Sericulture and Weaving.

Parliamentary Seat

Meghalaya has two Loksabha seats – one for Garo Hills and the other for Khasi-Jaintia Hills - and one Rajya sabha seat. All these parliamentary seats are absolutely reserved for the major hill tribes of the state.

Conclusion

It is already obvious that before the independence the Muslim leaders played leading role in the politics in the hilly region of present day Meghalaya as well as in the plains of Assam. Their contribution to the development of politics and economy of the hilly region cannot be belittled. The present generation Muslim leaders can also play an effective role in bringing further progress and prosperity of the state. The Muslims of the state have electoral strength to elect two-three representatives from among them in every Legislative Assembly election. If their elected representatives can form a solid block within an existing political party or outside it and remain honest and sincere, in this age of coalition politics they will be able to play still an important role in the state politics.

ENDNOTES

1. Rao V. Venkata & Hazarika Niru, A century of Government and politics in North-East India, Vol. 1, Assam (1874-1980), 1983, S. Chand & Company Ltd., Ram Nagar, New Delhi – 110055, P. 50.
2. Ibid, P. 52.
3. Report of the working of the Assam Legislative Assembly 1937 - 45, Shillong 1946, P. 1, cited in Dev B.J. & Lahiri D.K., Assam Muslims: Politics and Cohesion, Published by K.M. Mittal, Mittal Publictions, B-2 / 19-B, Lawrence Road, Delh i- 110035, P. 61.
4. Rao V. Venkata & Hazarika Niru, Op. Cit., PP. 58-59.
5. Dev B.J. & Lahiri D.K., Op. Cit., P. 120.
6. Nag Sajal, Roots of Ethnic Conflict: Nationality question in North-East India, 1990, Published by Ramesh Jain, Manohar Publications, 2/6 Ansari Road, Daryaganj, New Delhi – 110002, P. 126.
7. Rao V. Venkata & Hazarika Niru, Op. Cit., P. 64.
8. Bhattacharjee Arun, Assam in Indian Independence, 1993, Published by K.M. Rai Mittal for Mittal Publications, A – 110, Mohan Garden, New Delhi – 110059, P. 78.
9. Rao V. Venkata & Hazarika Niru, Op.Cit, P. 69.
10. Kar M., Muslims in Assam Politics, 1997,Vikas Publishing House Pvt. Ltd., 576 Masjid Road, Jangpura, New Delhi – 110014,P. 37.
11. Rao V. Venkata & Hazarika Niru, Op. Cit., P.84.
12. Kar M., Op. Cit., Pp. 37 – 38.
13. Ibid, P. 160.

CHAPTER VII

Influence of Islam on Tribal Life and Culture

Meghalaya contains winding chains of hills and mountain ranges, plateaus, waterfalls, rivers and lush green forests. Its hilly terrain had been, besides offering them shelter, isolating the hill tribes from the people of plains of Bengal and Assam and protecting them from the influence of the alien cultures for centuries. But because of their economic needs and their urge for development, the hill tribes had to establish and maintain contact with the people of the plains and even extend their settlement to the plain region of Bengal and Assam. Consequently, Hinduism, Islam and Christianity have, in course of time, influenced their life and culture, though in varied forms and degrees. Here an attempt is made to pin point the impact of Islam on the tribal societies.

Administrative and revenue system

Though the hilly region comprising today's Meghalaya was not conquered and ruled by the Muslim rulers of Bengal yet it could not remain free from the influence of their administrative and revenue system. In Jaintia kingdom *parganah* system was adopted in phases in adjoining areas of sarkar of Sylhet.[1] Jaintia king Ram Singh (1701-08) appointed a *Sikdar* in each village and *Choudhury* over sixteen *Sikdars*. The primary function of the *Choudhury* was to collect revenue for the king. The *Sikdar* and the *Choudhury* were bestowed with judicial power to settle the petty cases.[2] The Khasi kings whose states were extended to border of the *Sarkar* of Sylhet recruited *Mukhtars* for maintaining records and correspondences. The title of the village headman was given as *Matabar* and *Sirdar,* and meetings and the councils were called *Durbar*. The chiefs of the Shella areas took the title of *Wahaddars*.[3] According to Allen, in 1858 there were six *Wahadadars* in Shella areas.[4] In Garo Hills the British introduced the institution of the *Laskars*, *Sirdars* and *Zimmadars*. *Zimmadari* system was, however, abolished after one year of its introduction.[5] The institution of *Laskar* and *Sirdar* has been continuing to exist till to this day, besides the *Mouzadari* system in the western part of West Garo Hills. Thus many elements of Afghan and Mughal administration were introduced and assimilated in the tribal societies of Meghalaya. In Aain-e-Akbari Jaintia is mentioned as one of the eight *Mahals* of the *sarka*r of Sylhet. It is indicative of the fact that with the conquest of Sylhet in 1303 by Sikandar Gazi, the Muslim influence and their settlement in Jaintia considerably increased though Jaintia was left unconquered by the Muslim rulers of Bengal.

Racial fusion

It is already clear to us that the Muslim and the tribal people have been living together in the plains of Bengal and Assam as well as in the hills of Meghalaya for centuries. They were aware of the culture, religion, language, food, dress and the way of life of each other. Some tribal people used to send their children to the Muslim run school in the plains of Bengal. These children were exposed to the Islamic history, literature, Bengali language and culture. Some Muslim men married tribal women after converting them to their religion. Their children were taught Arabic and Urdu besides the languages of their parents. Thus a new generation of people in both Muslim and tribal communities through the fusion of the Muslim and tribal blood and culture came into existence. This was happened not only in the plains of Bengal and Assam but also in the hills. The founders of the *Siyem* clan of a Khasi state called Mawiong were the Bengali Muslims of Sylhet.[6] It is also said that the Momin clan of the Garos came into being as a consequence of the marriage of a Muslim man with a Garo woman. But some Garos do not like to subcribe to this view. However, the word, Momin, is the Arabic word which means believer. The Momin clan belongs to Awi, a division of the Garos. The Awi lived around a place called Damra that is situated in Goalpara district of Assam at the foot of present East Garo Hills district. Damra had been a centre of business for many years even before the advent of the Christian missionaries. The Garos used to exchange cotton, lac and their other Products for food grains and other products of the plain belt at Damra market. The Muslim traders had visited the market. It is probable that some of them established matrimonial relationship with the Garos and founded the Momin clan. Many Muslims have been living in Damra till today. The origin of these Muslims can be traced to such intermarriages. The contact between the Muslims and the tribal people was more or less peaceful and their influence on each other was reciprocal.

Languuage

The Khasis, Jaintias and the Garos were familiar with Bengali language. They used to write their respective mother tongue in Bengali script before learning the roman script from the Christian missionaries. It is probable that they had also some knowledge of the eastern Bengali dialect known as the Musalmani dialect. The eastern Bengali language was, perhaps, called Musalmani dialect, because majority of the Muslims of that region spoke it and it contained many Arabic, Persian, Urdu, Pushtu etc. words. The Musalmani dialect was spoken in Mymensing, Faridpur and Tippera.[7] The upcountry immigrants and a large number of respectable Muslim families of Dhaka spoke in Hindustani Language.[8] The tribal traders who visited Dhaka, Murshidabad, Calcutta etc. and maintained business connection with the Muslim traders had probably some knowledge of the Hindustani or Urdu, besides Bengali language.

Land documents of the Jaintia kingdom were written in Assamese and Bengali. "... The archives have revealed the existence of the land revenue records inscribed in the above characters and even in Persian and Arabic..."[9] "Familiarity with these scripts was obviously confined to the court, in particular to the scribes employed in it and probably started in 16th century"[10] This again shows that the Jaintia kings appointed the Muslim and Hindu officials alike in the courts and land revenue department. The use of Arabic, Persian, Bengali and Assamese was necessary, because the Khasi and Jaintia states had to correspond with the Muslim rulers of Bengal and the Ahom monarchs and their officials in the matter of trade and foreign affairs, and also with the private traders of Assam and Bengal.

During the Muslim rule in India " Turkish, Arabic, Persian and Urdu words have been assimilated in Hindi, Bengali, Gujrati and Marathi languages."[11] Persian had been the official language of India until 1835. Arabic, Persian and Turkish languages were widely used in royal families and courts and in writing history, travelogue and verses etc. Since the Bengali was widely used in the hilly region under reference, a good number of words of Islamic origin had found place in the vocabulary of the tribal languages through it. It may be pointed out here that "Through the efforts of the Muslim rulers of Bengal, Bengali came into its own"[12] During the British period a good number of Hindi, Bengali, Nepali, Assamese and Urdu speaking Muslim people came to the hilly region as government employees, businessmen, contractors, and as petty service providers of different professions from different parts of India. Even moneylenders from Afganistan locally known as *Cabliwala* came to this region. While these different language speakers learnt the local dialects and maintained contact with the local tribes in the interest of their professions, the hill tribes also became familiar with the different alien languages. In the process many words of Islamic origin found place in the vocabulary of tribal languages. A list of some such words, which are found even today in the principal tribal languages, is given in

Table 24.

Table 24: Words of Islamic Origin in Tribal Languages

Islamic origin	Khasi / Jaintia	Garo
Ain / Kanun (Law)	Ain-Kanun	-
Baniya (Grain merchant)	Bania	-
Ba'zar (Market)	Ba'zar	
Dawai (Medicine)	Dawai	-
Dag (Stain)	-	Dagi
Hukum (Order)	Hukum	Hukum
Hakim (Judge)	-	Hakim
Jawab (Response)	Jubab	-
Jora (Pair)	Jura	-
Karkhana (Workshop)	Karkhana	Karkhana
Khabar (News)	Khubor	Kobor
Kitab (Book)	Kitab	Kitab
qaidi (Prisoner)	Koid / Koidi	-
Naksha (Picture)	-	Noksha
Sahib (Authority)	Saheb	Saib / Saheb
Salam (Greeting)	-	Salam
Shaitan	Soitan	Satan
Tanka (Rupee)	Tyngka	Tanka
Tarikh	Tarik	Tarik
Tupi	Tupia / Tuprei	-
Wokil (Lawyer)	Ukil	-

"Mention may also be made that it were the Muslims who introduced paper in India"[13] With the introduction of paper and at the encouragement and patronization of the Muslim rulers of India, scholars of both Hindu and Muslim communities produced a great number of books of far reaching influence in Urdu, Hindi, Persian, Bengali and other vernacular languages in different subjects of human interests. This literary development might have influenced a section of the tribal population particularly that group who knew Bengali and visited different parts of Bengal for business and educational purposes. They might have made them familiar with some words of Islamic origin for the purpose of making their communication easy with the Muslim traders, scholars, physician, employees of the Khasi and Jaintia states and the common Muslim people at the time of need. A list of some more words of Islamic origin that found in the major tribal languages of Meghalaya is given in APPENDIX H.

Literature

As the hill tribes learnt the Bengali dialect and adopted many words of Islamic origin into their vocabulary, the Muslims settled in the hills learnt how to speak, read and write in tribal languages. Many of them even acquired the skill required to compose verses in the tribal languages. One such man is Sheikh Muhammad Amjad Ali. He has created history by composing poetry in Khasi language and earned the distinction of being first poet in Khasi language. The name of his first poetical work is "Ka Myntoi" (The Profit). It was first published from Calcutta in 1888. The Khasi Authors Society of Meghalaya reprinted the poetry book in 1980. As many as six poems of Amjad Ali have been so far included in the higher secondary school syllabus of Meghalaya (See Appendix D).

Of late, a number of books highlighting the different aspects of Islam is written in or translated into Khasi language and published by the Muslim intellectuals. These books have enriched the coffer of Khasi vocabulary and literatures. They are enlisted below for the sake of posterity:

1. Salah: Ka kot Jingduwai, published by Seng Bhalang Islam, Shillong.
2. Janghikai Ha Ka Islam (Translation of Talimul Islam), published by Seng Bhalang Islam, Shillong.
3. Niam Tynrai Bala Pynjanai: Islam, By M.A. Hydar, B. Com., B. Ed., Published by the author himself on behalf of Amjad Ali Foundation, Shillong.
4. U Nonglam Khubor (Ha ka ba Kut), A Translation of Prof. R. Rao's The Messenger of Allah, by M.A. Hydar & Bah Akbar Syimlieh, published by the Meghalaya Muslim Students' Union, Shillong.
5. U Jisu Christ ha ka Bhalang ki Muslim, Published by Amjad Ali Foundation, Shillong.
6. Bat kiwei kiwei, Published by Amjad Ali Foundation, Shillong.
7. Ka Qur'an Bakhuid, A Khasi translation of the Holy Qur'an by M.A. Hydar, 2002, published by the Board of Islamic Publication, North-East branch, Hidayetpur, Guwahati.
8. Ka Myntoi, By Sheikh Muhammad Amjad Ali, 1888. Calcutta.

Economy

The main occupation of the hill people of Meghalaya in the pre-colonial period was agriculture. The Method of land cultivation was primitive. Coming into contact with the Muslim peasants of Bengal, the tribal people particularly those who are settled in the plains at the foot of the hills learnt the use of plough and cultivation of new crops, fruits and vegetables.

With the appearance of the Muslim traders in the hills, the volume of trade between the hills and the plains increased. Prior to the establishment of Mughal rule in Bengal, all business transactions were carried out on the basis of barter system. The Mughal traders used to visit markets and religious fairs that took place at the foot of the hills. "S*icca Tanka* which was unit of circulation in medieval Bengal, was obviously the common media."[14] This shows the tribal traders learnt the use money as a medium of exchange from the Muslim traders of Bengal. Thus their barter economy of old gradually started to transform into money economy. They still call money *Tyngka.*

Under the influence of the Mughal traders, contractors and technicians, the industries in the hills began to develop in terms of quality, technique and productivity. The Mughals took keen interest in raising the production, quality and volume of trade of limes by employing new technique and method for the development of lime quarries.

Dress

The hill men have slowly and gradually adopted the western dress code with their subjugation by the British in the early part of the 19th century as the culture of the ruler in the initiative of the Christian missionaries. Now-a-days a very few men folk of the Khasi-Pnars wear their traditional dresses like *Jainboh* (Dhuti), *Soptipoh* (Shirt) etc. They do not wear *Jaingphong* (A kind of waist coat) and *Jaingspong* (Turban) any more except in their traditional religious festivals. The practice of wearing turban was perhaps started under the influence of Turk-Afgan rulers of Bengal. The Garo men wore very scanty cloth. However, the tribal women have retained their traditional dresses that have now improved to great a extent in quality, art and design. Of late the use of *Salwar*, *Kamiz* and *Sari* is also becoming popular among them because of the influence of television and cinema as well as their increasing contact in different aspects of life with the Muslims and Hindus of other parts of the country. The use of *Kurta* and *Payjama* also are gradually becoming popular among the hill men.

Ornament

The tribal women commonly wear ornaments like necklace, earring and finger ring. They also use bracelet and bangle occasionally. Nowadays their traditional ornaments are improved a lot in design and art because of outside influence. The Muslim jewellers of Shillong are said to have played an important role in improving quality and design of their ornaments while keeping their traditional elements of the ornaments intact.

Architecture

Islamic art and architecture is introduced in the hilly region with the construction of mosque, tombs, *dargahs* and *Madarasahs*. However, the region can not claim to have any finest Islamic monument like that of other parts of India as it was never a part of the Muslim rule. Muslim mason and carpenters are mainly responsible for introduction of some elements of Islamic art and architectural designs in the region.

Personal hygiene

The conception of Islamic hygiene has also influenced the

life of the tribal people to a great extend. This influence is quite noticeable in the matter of taking bath at regular interval, washing mouth and hand before and after taking food, private parts with water after attending nature's call and cleaning teeth, tongue, nostrils and throat.

Food

The food habits of the tribal people are simple. They usually eat boiled meat, fish both dry and fresh and vegetables with rice. However, because of the Muslim and Christian influences, new items of food, fruits and new style of cookery are introduced in many tribal homes. The tribal people, who have come into the fold of Islam, abstain from taking pork and alcohol. The Khasis and Jaintias continually chew betel nut and leaf with lime.

Conclusion

The Muslims, the Hindus and different tribal communities have been living together for centuries in the north-East India particularly in the hilly region of present day Meghalaya and influencing thought, language, culture, life style and economic activity of each other for the sake of their mutual peaceful co-existence and development. "The close contacts and understanding between the peoples resulted in progressive assimilation of the immigrants of different faiths. The immigrants ... contributed substantial elements towards the growth of new technology, art and crafts in the region as a whole. In course of time, the lone words crept in local languages and myriad tribal dialects while food and dress habits of the people underwent transformation."[15]

ENDNOTES

1. Dutta Sushil Chandra. The North-East and the Mughals (1661 – 1714). 1984. D.K. Publications. New Delhi – 110007. Pp. 212 & 218. Ali S.M., The History of Jaintia. P. 25.

2. Gurdon P.R., The Khasis. Pp. 75 – 91. cited in Dutta Sushil Chandra. Op. Cit. P. 219.

3. Chatterji S.K.,Kirta-Jana-Krti,P 86, cited in Dutta Sushil Chandra, Ibid.

4. Rao V. Venkata, Pakem B., Hazarika N., A Century of Government and Politics in North-East India, Vol. II, Meghalaya (1874 – 1983), 1984, S. Chand & Company Ltd., New Delhi – 110055, P. 77

5. Ibid, Pp. 74-75.

6. Herbert D., Succession to Syiemship in Khasi states, P 32, cited in Dutta P. N., Relations of the Khasis and Jaintias with their southern neighbours till the British intervention, paper presented in the first session of North-East India History Associtionm, Shillong, 1'980, P. 79.

7. BCA, EAG, HFH & CGHA, Gazetteer of Bengal and North-East India, 2001, Mittal Publications, New Dehli – 110059, Pp. 325, 342 & 376.

8. Ibid, P. 300.

9. Bareh Hamlet, Progress of education in Meghalaya, 1996, Cosmo Publications for Genesis Publishing Pvt. Ltd., Ansari Road, Daryaganj, New Delhi, P. 151.

10. Meghalaya District Gazetter: Jaintia Hills, 1996, edited by I.M.Simon, Government of Meghalaya, Arts and Culture Department, Meghalaya, Shillong, p. 181.

11. Luniya B. N., Evolution of Indian culture. 1990, Lakshmi Narain Agarwal Educational Publications, Agra – 3, P. 421.

12. Ibid. P. 331.

13. Ibid. P. 421.

14. Bhattacharjee J.B.. Cachar under British rule in North-East India. P. 207. cited in Dutta Sushil Chandra. Op. Cit.. P. 227.

15. Dutta Sushil Chandra. Op.Cit. P. 244

CHAPTER VIII

Muslim economic situation

Meghalaya is basically an agrarian state. Eighty-three per cent of its population is dependent on agriculture for their livelihood. As per survey conducted by the National Sample Survey (NSS) covering a period from July 1999 to June 2000, a total of 8.23 lakh people of Meghalaya live below the poverty line. The economic condition of the Muslims of the state is no way better than that of their tribal counterpart. The Muslim constitutes 3.46 per cent of the state's total population. Over 70 per cent of them depend on agriculture for earning their livelihood. The rest of their population is engaged in different trades and professions.

Agricultural Labourers

There is a good number of labourers among the Muslim people who depend on agriculture for their livelihood. They are mostly landless people. They are economically the most disadvantaged group of the Muslim population. They work as daily wage earner for those who hire them for earning their livelihood. A number of this work force migrates to urban and sub-urban areas in search of jobs every year and live temporarily for three to five months in a year in slum areas in a very unhygienic condition. They mainly work as carpenter, mason or labourer in government or private construction sites. However, they are playing an important role in the construction and development of roads, buildings and bridges in the state. Literacy rate among these people is miserably low.

Farmers

The economic plight of the Muslim farmers is far from satisfactory. The total area of land available for cultivation to each farmer is very small, fragmented and divided into small plots. The farmer cannot buy any land for cultivation or other purposes as law in the state prohibits transfer of land to the non-tribal people. Moreover, agricultural crops are often damaged by flood or draught. Only a few fortunate farmers get to eat two square meals a day.

Muslim employment

Only a small section of the Muslims are employed in government services. 95 percent of the government jobs are reserved for the scheduled tribes and other backward tribes. Only 5 per cent jobs are left unreserved for the general category of candidates. Since the vacancies for jobs are very limited, very few Muslim educated youth get recruitment in the government sector. Since the creation of Meghalaya in 1972, not a single Muslim could make it to the state civil services. Out of the total of 8271 police personnel in the state, number of Muslims is only 159. Their representation in the state police department is only 1.9 percent.[1]

According to Meghalaya Government Employees Census Report the total number of Meghalaya employees was 46, 529 as on March 31, 2000. 84.95 per cent of them belonged to the Scheduled Tribe, 1.52 percent to the Scheduled Caste and 3.17 percent to the other backward classes and 10.36 percent belong to others.[2] Religion wise number or percentage of employees is not reflected in the census report. Therefore, clear picture of the representation of the religious minorities in the state government sector is not available. But it is understandable that the percentage of Muslim employees of the total employees of the state will not be more than two per cent. It is far below the percentage of their population (3.46) to the state's total population.

Muslim representation in the various central government departments located in the state is also very poor. Their representation in the banking sector in the state is negligible.

Enterprise

Since farming has not been dependable and profitable and there has been hardly any chance of getting employment in the government and semi-government sectors, the Muslims of the state are now gradually taking up trade and commerce as their profession. They are seen running their own business establishment like cloth shop, pharmacy, bookstall, tea stall, biscuit shop, grocery and stationary shops etc. in different towns in the state.

Some of the Muslims are also gradually setting up their own industrial ventures like rice mill, bakery, brick making, tailoring, motor garage, scooter and cycle repairing shops, radio and TV repairing shops, furniture making etc. A small number of Muslims are also working as contractors and running private bus and taxi services. A good number of educated youth has been working as teachers in private or government aided schools or colleges on a nominal salary in different parts of the state.

Muslim localities

It is said that the transport is the bearer of civilization and prosperity of man. But the Muslim inhabited areas of West Garo Hills district are the most backward areas in road and transport communication in the state. The construction of permanent road connecting all villages could not been undertaken as these localities are affected by flood every year. It would be difficult to construct and maintain road without taking up suitable flood control measure in these flood prone areas.

The state government has set up a number of health centers, animal heath care centers, banks, post offices etc. in the adjoining areas of the Muslim inhabited localities. But the fruit of this development could not reach the needy people properly as the people are not well aware of the schemes offered by the developmental agencies.

However, almost all the Muslim inhabited villages are also furnished by electricity and telephone connections. But the people could not exploit the facilities for their socio-economic advancement because of their educational and economic backwardness. Out of the state's total estimated Muslim population of 83, 487 only 578 persons[3] had telephone connection in the state in 2000. This speaks volume of the socio-economic condition of the Muslims of Meghalaya.

The lack of Education, knowledge of different trades and avenues for employment is the main reason of the backwardness of the Muslims living in the state. In view of this there is an urgent need for establishment of an Industrial Training Institute for the Muslim youth to equip them with necessary knowledge, information and skill to enable them to establish different cottage and small-scale industries and give much needed boost to the state's economy.

Changing the Muslim situation

It appears that the present plight of the Meghalaya Muslims can only be improved through proper education and training. The Muslim of every locality should come forward to mobilize their locally available resources and endevour to establish and run nursery and primary schools in their respective area so that all children in their locality can at least know how to read and write in their mother tongue with understanding, besides receiving their religious education. While new Madarasahs and schools will be set up to cater the educational need of the community, the existing Madarasahs should be upgraded and subjects like mathematics, science and vocational courses in addition of teaching of theology should be included in the Madrasah curriculum. Those students who opted for general education and dropped out may be motivated and admitted into the Madarasahs located in their locality. The ultimate objective of the community should be to " produce the required number of relevant philosophers, social and natural scientists and writers who are actively engaged in explaining and guiding the destinies of that community or nation. There should be a large cadres of thinkers, scholars and researchers who understand and guide societal dynamics of that community in the context of the nation and the world in both historical perspective and futuristic projection."[4]

The Muslim educated youth should come forward in a big way to set up their own commercial enterprise and strive to become self-reliant. They should not depend on the government alone for their employment. No government can provide employment to all of its citizens. The Holy Qur'an and the Holy prophet (peace be upon him) have, therefore, exhorted the believers to take up trade and commerce as their professions. The Holy Qur'an says: " He (Allah) brought you forth from the earth and settled you therein to develop,"[5] "Believers! Do not devour one another's possessions wrongfully; rather than that, let there be trading by mutual consent" [6] and "Allah hath permitted trading and forbideth usury."[7] " It is the pious duty of the Muslims to undertake commercial activities to earn wealth and spend it to meet the requirement of their religion and society." [8]

"The only occupation that the Prophet (peace be upon him) followed, other than his prophetic duties was trade. That the trade is a superior way of earning one's livelihood." [9] This is clear from these sayings [10] of the Holy Prophet (peace be upon him): "If you profit by doing what is permitted, thy deed is a *jihad* and, if thou uses it for the family and kindred, this will be a *sadaqah* (pious work of charity)." "Truly a *dirham* (silver coin) lawfully gained from trade is worth more than 10 *dirhams* gained in any other way." " The merchant who is sincere and trustworthy will (on the Day of Judgement) be alongwith the Prophets, the pious and the martyrs."

"Islam exhorts people to acquire knowledge in science, technology and theology, because such knowledge enables a man to improve his earning skill and ability, to perform his religious duties with devotion and sincerity"[11] and thus, to achieve success in the world and the Hereafter. Now-a-days books on different trades and professions are available in plenty in the market. The Muslim educated youth can buy the books of their chosen trade and acquire the required knowledge and skill to start their own economic enterprise. " Every Muslim is under obligation to work in order to live, and no body is entitled to any gain or reward without exerting a productive effort or shouldering subsequent risk."[12]

Conclusion

The root cause of the socio-economic backwardness of the Meghalaya Muslims is their illiteracy. It should be the first priority of the community to remove the curse of their illiteracy by making education for all a social movement. Education can only empower the community to solve their all problems by their own effort and action. It can only increase their knowledge, develop better understanding of their problems, bring co-operation among them, enhance their skill and help them to improve the quality of their services and products and raise their income and standard of living. There is no alternative path of development of the community except education. Education is a continuous process. It starts at the birth of a person and continues till he or she enters paradise.

The importance of education can be understood from the fact that the first *surah* revealed by Allah asked the Holy Prophet (pbuh) neither to establish worship nor to construct a mosque for the purpose but to read thus:

Read! In the name of thy Lord Who createth,
Created man from a clot.
Read! And thy Lord is the Most bounteous,
who taught by the pen,
Taught man that which he knew not.[13]

ENDNOTES

1. Sultana Nargis, Police role in communal riots, Radiance Viewsweekly, 17-23 January 1999, P. 41.
2. Report on Census of Meghalaya state Government employees as on 31st March 2000, Govrnment of Meghalaya, Directorate of Economics & Statistics, Shillong, P. 1.
3. Computed from the Meghalaya Telephone Directory 2000.
4. Khan M.A. Saleem, Muslim decline in India in The Muslim Situation in India, 1989 edited by Iqbal A. Ansari, Sterling Publishers Pvt. Ltd., New Delhi – 110016, P. 78.
5. The Holy Qur'an, Surah XI: Ayah 61.
6. Ibid, Surah IV: Ayah 29.
7. Ibid, Surah II: Ayah 275.
8. Rahman Mohammad Hasibor, Economic Principles of Islam, Muslim & Arab Perspective, Vol. 4, Issue 7 – 12, February 1999, P. 287.
9. Akbar M., Entrepreneurship and Indian Muslims, 1990, Nanak Publications Pvt. Ltd., New Delhi – 110002, P. 8.
10. Cited in Ibid.
11. Rahman Mohammad Hasibor, Op. Cit. P. 288.
12. Akbar M. OP.Cit. P. 12.
13. The Holy Qur'an, Surah XCVI: Ayah 1 – 5.

CHAPTER IX

Muslim religious and educational institutions

It appears that the Muslims of this hilly region of today's Meghalaya performed their prayers at their homes individually and in temporary shades collectively in the beginning of their settlement. Their children were taught at the houses of their religious leaders and in the Muktab attached to the place of their worship. There is no ancient monument in the state except five tombs known to be of Mir Jumlah, Shah Kamal, Shah Nur Muhammad Shah, Shah Shafreen Shah and Sayed Sulaiman Chisti Sabri Masoom Shah.

The tomb of Mir Jumlah

Mir Jumlah was a very brave and intelligent general of emperor Aurangzeb (1658 – 1707). Aurangzeb appointed him as the Nawab of Bengal and Bihar. Mir Jumlah conquered Koch Bihar in 1661 and the entire Ahom kingdom including its capital at Garhgaon in 1662. While returning to Dhaka after the conquest of Assam, he fell seriously ill and died on March 30, 1663 before reaching Dhaka.[1] According to oral tradition, he died at a hilltop located at the Assam-Meghalaya border near Mankachar. Before his death he took rest at the hilltop for days with his associates and constructed a mosque there. The mosque is known as the Mir Jumlah mosque. It is, however, renovated or reconstructed several times and existing till to this day by the side of his grave. The Muslims living around the hilltop have been using it for worship.

The tomb of Shah Kamal

It is said that Shah Kamal, a Muslim saint, visited the Garo Hills and stayed at a place near Indo-Bangla border in Mahendraganj at the request of a Garo Chief and married a daughter of a Hindu Brahmin. He was a very pious and spiritually enlightened man and well known for helping people in distress and preaching the message of Islam among the local people. The legend has it that one day he suddenly disappeared from this place and after some years of his disappearance two graves appeared at the place where he stayed before. Then people began to believe that one grave is of Shah Kamal and the other grave to be of his wife. Except this legend, very little is known about him.

In this connection it may be noted that at the time of his expedition to Assam in 1669, Mughal general Ram Singh brought five Muslim saints with him. They were Shah Akbar, Shah Bagmar, Shah Charan, Shah Sufi and Shah Kamal. After their death, they were buried in Dhubri at a place that is known till today as the *Dargah* of *Panch Pirs*.[2] It is probable that Shah Kamal who accompanied Ram Singh might have visited Garo Hills and stayed at Mahendraganj for some times for the purpose of helping people and preaching Islam among them.

The tomb of Shah Nur Muhammad Shah

This grave is located at Laban in Shillong. But the local

people, when contacted, could not throw much light on the deceased Muslim saint. However, a person informed that the grave is of Shah Nur Muhammad Shah and renovated and developed by a non-Muslim politician about one and half decades back.[3] The General Secretary of the Shillong Muslim Union told that Shah Nur Muhammad Shah was one of the disciples of Shah Jalal, the famous 14th century Muslim saint of Sylhet.[4] Shah Jalal came to India from Yemen.

The tomb of Shah Safreen Shah

The stone tomb of Shah Safreen Shah is situated about half a kilometre away from Bangladesh border on a hill located on the east bank of river Umngot near Dawki suspension bridge constructed in 1931 by Kumar Dhubi Engineering Limited at a distance of about 95 kilometres from Shillong. The tomb falls in the area of Umsyiem village of East Khasi Hills district. According to legend, two Muslim saints came to the locality by boat from Sylhet and lived and died there. Among the local people they were known as *Phukir*. The stone where they were buried is still locally known as the *Maw Phukir* meaning stone of *Phukir*.[5] When I visited the spot I have seen only one stone grave on one side of which is written the name of Hajrad Shah Safreen Shah. The grave is renovated in 2000 and this is recorded by writing only 2000 with white paint on a rock near the grave.

On the way a few metres away before reaching the stone grave of Shah Safreen Shah the grave of one Imam of Dawki mosque named Ali is situated. At the time of my visit the grave was covered with a piece of green cloth. The Meghalaya Waqf Board of has been taking care of both the graves. According to the Secretary of the Waqf Board, Shah Safreen Shah was also a disciple of Shah Jalal, the renowned saint of Sylhet.[6]

The tomb of Masoom Shah

Sayed Sulaiman Chisti Sabri Masoom Shah was a pathan from Afghanistan. He came to Lucknow at his early life and stayed there for some years. He married in Lucknow and then migrated to Shillong and settled at Thana Road, Police Bazar from where he helped people who are sick and in distress and need of spiritual guidance. He commanded respect from all sections of people in Shillong. He died in 1957 and buried at Mewprem Muslim graveyard.

Mosque

The mosque is the most revered institution of Muslim worship and learning. There are a good number of mosques in the state of Meghalaya. Names of as many as fifty-three mosques* have been collected and their district-wise position is shown as in Table 25.

Table 25: District-wise location of mosques in Meghalaya

Name of district	Location of Mosque	Date of Establishment
East Khasi Hills	1. Police Bazar	In the 3rd quarter of 19th century
	2. Garikhana	1896
	3. Laban	1818, renovated in 1942
	4. Laitumkhrah	1942
	5. Bara pathar	Reconstructed in 2003
Jaintia Hills	1. Dawki	In the 1st quarter of 20th century
Ri Bhoi	1. Umbneng	-
	2. Nongpoh	-
	3. Byrnihat	-
East Garo Hills	1. William Nagar Town mosque	1986
	2. William Nagar Bazar mosque	1999
	3. Rongjeng	-
West Garo Hills	1. Mir Jumlah	1663
	2. Tura Town	-
	3. Singimari	-
	4. Sobribari	-
	5. Rajabala	-
	6. Sakmal	-
	7. Sidakandi	-
	8. Old Bhaitbari	-
	9. New Bhaitbari	-
	10. Belbari	-
	11. Nayagaon	-

Name of district	Location of Mosque	Date of Establishment
West Garo Hills	12. Haripur	Hills
	13. Garodubi	-
	14. Gomai Jhora	-
	15. Phulbari	-
	16. Bholarvita	-
	17. Chibinang	-
	18. Kalaichar	-
	19. Mahendraganj (Bazar)	-
	20. Moulakandi	-
	21. Haribhaga	-
	22. Tikrikilla	-
	23. Charbatapara	-
	24. Bangalkata Babupara	-
	25. Goladingri	-
	26. Patharkata	-
	27. Kazipara	-
	28. Khanpara	-
	29. Tungrurchar – I	-
	30. Tungrurchar – II	-
	31. Qaripara – I	-
	32. Qaripara – II	-
	33. Qamarpara	-
	34. Bagicha	-
	35. Kukurmua Saglipara	-
	36. Mondalpara	-
	37. Ghegapara	-
	38. Nandirchar	-
	39. Sandarpara	-
	40. Nukairchar	-
	41. Dughoripara	-

All five mosques of East Khasi Hills are located within the capital town of Shillong. The mosque located at Laban is the first mosque of Shillong. The Police Bazar mosque is situated at Thana Road. Hazi Qasimuddin had established the mosque on his own land.

Dawki mosque is the oldest mosque in the district of Jaintia Hills. It is located in Dawki Bazar near the Indo-Bangla border.

The mosques situated in West Garo Hills district are very old in origin. Many of them are established many years before the advent of the British in Garo Hills. The mosques were made of bricks and thatches. The British chroniclers recorded this thus: "Mohammedan mosques are usually small brick structures, consisting of an open quadrangle with a covered archade at the west end; but in some remoter parts of the province, service is held in thatched hut."[7] Now almost all the mosques are reconstructed and renovated into beautiful buildings.

Idgah

Eid is the most revered and popular religious festival of the Muslims. There are two Muslim Eids – *Eid-ul-Fitr* and *Eid-ul-Azha*. *Eid-ul-Fitr* is observed on the first day of the Arabic month of *Shawwa*l following one month of fasting during Ramadan and *Eid-ul-Azha* on the 10th day of the month of *Zil-Hajj*. The open field where congregational prayer is offered on the occasion of *Eid* is called *Idgah*. The list of the places where some Idgahs* in the state are located is given in Table 26.

Table 26: District-wise location of Idgah in Meghalaya

West Garo Hills	East Khasi Hills	East Garo Hills
1. Tura	1. Laban	1. William Nagar
2. Rajabala	2. Laitumkhrah	
3. Haripur	3. Mawprem	
4. New Bhaitbari		
5. Old Bhaitbari		
6. Phulbari		
7. Sobribari		
8. Belbari		
9. Naya para		
10. Chibinang		
11. Moulakandi		
12. Bholarvita (Haguragaon)		
13. Mir Jumlah		
14. Nandirchar		
15. Tungrurchar		
16. Majherchar – II		
17. Nukairchar		

Graveyard

The Muslims bury their dead body with due respect in a place that is allocated as their community graveyard after giving bath to dead body and performing the necessary funeral rites. The funeral prayer is a common obligation on all Muslims of the locality to which the deceased belongs. The location of some known Muslim graveyards* of the state is compiled in Table 27.

Table 27: District-wise Location of Muslim Graveyards

West Garo Hills	East Khasi Hills East	Garo Hills
1. Tura	1. Lumparing (Laban)	1. William Nagar
2. Haripur	2. Mawprem	
3. Chibinang	3. Bara pathar	
4. Saglipara		

Madrasah

Madrasah is the profoundly respected centre of learning of the Muslims. It has been incessantly spreading light of knowledge in the world of darkness over 1400 years. History is the witness that the products of the madrasah have played the leading role in the development of the modern civilization of the world. They had removed darkness from Europe and civilized it. In the independence movement of India, they were in the forefront and source of inspiration of millions of people. The books written by them have been serving as an invaluable original source of knowledge.

Madaris are found in every nook and corner of every Muslim inhabited region of the world. In Meghalaya there are also a number of Madaris* in the Muslim inhabited localities. Name, location and date of establishment of some of them are given in Table 28.

Table 28: Madaris of Meghalaya

Sl	Name of Madrasahs	Location	Date of establishment
1	Himayat–ul-Islam	Garikhana,	Shillong 1953
2	Darul Ulum Keramatia Madrasah	Moulakandi Under Phulbari LAC	-
3	Khariji Muktab	Mahendraganj	-
4	Darul Ulum Madrasah	New Bhaitbari	1988
5.	Garodubi-Magurmari Mansuria Madrasah	Garodubi	1958
6.	Darul Maa Qariana Madrasah	Nalbari	1977
7	Hafjul Qur'an Siddiqia Madrasah	Mir Jumlah	1985

Conclusion

There is a great need for efficient management of all the existing Muslim institutions of the state. Construction of boundary walls of the graveyards and Idgahs is required to avoid encroachment and unwanted litigation. The Muslims of Meghalaya are in need of their own dispensary, technical educational institution, orphanage, library, literary organization and the like. Muslim leaders and intellectuals should come forward and joined their hands together for the development of their community utilizing the locally available resources.

ENDNOTES

1. Gait E., A History of Assam, 1984, LBS Publications, Guwahati, Assam, P. 103.

2. Ahmad Mohammad Muhiuddin, Asomloi Musolmanor Agamon Aaru Sanscritic Songmisron, 2000, Published by Begum A. Akhtar, Anandanagar, Panigaon, Nagaon, P. 13.

3. Hussain Zakir, Howall Road, Laban, Shillong – 4, dated 22 – 10 – 2001.

4. Nongrum Sayeed Ullah, Bisnupur, Shillong, dated 01 – 12 – 2002.

5. (i) Rangdong Livingstone, Village: Umsyiem in East Khasi Hills district, dated 18 – 11 – 2002.

(ii) Suchen Rombar, Village: Darrang, Jaintia Hills district, dated 18–11-2002.

6. Nongrum Sayeed Ullah, Op. Cit.

7. BCA, EAG, HFW & CGHA, Gazetteer of Bengal and North-East India, 2001, Mittal Publications, A – 110, Mohan Garden, New Delhi – 110059, P. 55.

* Information about mosques, Idgahs, Graveyards and Madariss of Meghalaya are provided by the following persons:

i. Sarkar Abdul Motin, Village & P.O. Haripur, West Garo Hills.

ii. Hoque Sulaiman, Village: Goladigli, Moulakandi, West Garo Hills.

iii. Karim Rezaul, Village: Majherchar, P.O. Mahendraganj, West Garo Hills.

iv. Sheikh Abdus Sobur, Village: Garodubi, P.O. Rajabala, West Garo Hills.

v. Begum Mt. Latifa, Nongrim Hills, Shillong.

vi. Muhammad Ayat, Nongrim Hills, Shillong.

Epilogue

The Muslims of Meghalaya are mostly, like the Muslims of other parts of India, the descendents of the converts of different scheduled castes and scheduled tribes of the hilly region and the plains lying at its foot. They are divided into different lingual groups. But their religion has bound them into a broad homogenous cultural group.

The Muslims living in the state can be classified into four economic groups such as (i) Farmers, (ii) Skilled, semi-skilled and unskilled labourers, (iii) White-collared professionals. (iv) Traders and entrepreneurs and The farmers and labourers are socio-economically at the bottom of the ladder of development.

The main problems of the Muslims of the state are (i) unemployment, (ii) illiteracy, (iii) intellectual backwardness, (iv) low rate of saving and capital formation, and (v) lack of opportunity of investment.

It is the fact that it would not be possible for the government to provide employment to its all unemployed manpower particularly that of the Muslim community. 95 per cent of the government jobs are reserved in the ratio of 40 per cent for the Khasi-Jaintias. 40 per cent for the Garos and 15 per cent for the other backward classes. Only 5 per cent jobs are left unreserved. The Muslims constitute 3.46 per cent of the total population of state. Their representation to the gevernment service would not be more than two per cent. They can raise the demand for granting them the status of Other Backward Caste and representation to the government services in proportion to their population. If the demand is fulfilled, this will provide some relief to the community but not solve its unemployment problem totally. The state is industrially backward and therefore, there is no question of getting job in the private sectors. The Muslim educated youth should not depend only on government jobs. They should come forward to establish their own business and commercial enterprise with the resources available at their disposal. Small cottage industries can provide good opportunity of employment for them and their family members and friends. Setting up of large industrial unit in the beginning would be difficult for them, even if they have their own capital to do so. Because they will not be able to buy land in proper site to establish their industrial venture as the non-tribal people are barred from purchasing land in the state. Moreover, the future of their venture will remain uncertain because of insecure atmosphere caused by rising insurgency among the tribal youths in the state. The opportunity of investment in the private sectors is very limited.

As there is acute shortage of cultivable land in the possession of the Muslim farmers and its area can not be increased, the Muslim farmars are left with no alternative but to adopt multiple cropping system of high yielding crops to put their land, manpower and other resources in proper use. It is also necessary to replace the traditional farming with improved techniques such as the use of improved variety of seeds, fertilizers and effective plant protection measures. This will go a long way in improving their economic condition besides giving much needed impetus to the state's economy.

It is high time for the Muslim of Meghalaya to eradicate the curse of illiteracy from their community. Muktabs and Madarasahs can play vital role in removing illiteracy and enlightening the mind of the ignorant people with knowledge at a very low cost at their doorstep. Many Madarasahs provide free lodging and food. The poor parents can send their children to these Madaris and get their children educated without bearing much financial burden. The Madarasahs educated people can get employment easily as teacher, Imam, Muezzin and Qazi. They can also work as preacher, healer, Qari, writer, counsellor, private tutor or establish and run their own business enterprise or educational institution in their own locality. All parents cannot afford to send their all children to the government run schools as they are unable to bear expenses for books, uniform, tuition, admission and examination fees etc. in addition to food and dress because of their poor economic status. The convenient way of removing illiteracy from the Muslim society is to establish Islamic Nursery, Muktab and Madrasah in every Muslim village or locality. The educational curriculum must include at least one vocational course like tailoring, bamboo, cane and wooden furniture or other household article making, gardening, poultry etc. that can be undertaken with locally available resources. The products can be sold in the market and the profit can be utilized for the welfare of the institution and students. Thus the students can be equipped with necessary knowledge and skill to be self-reliant in their future life.

Learning is a continuous process. It begins at birth and come to an end only when a person enters paradise. This is obvious from this saying of the Holy Prophet (peace be upon him): " A believer never stop seeking of knowledge till he (or she) enters paradise" (Tirmidhi). The Muslim teachers, Preachers, politicians and religious leaders, particularly the Imams are regarded as the thinker, philosopher and guide of their community. They should always remember the precious teaching of the holy Prophet (peace be upon him) and constantly endeavour to acquire all kinds of useful knowledge and be aware of the socio-economic, technological and political changes taking place in and around them and provide right kind of guidance, direction and leadership to their community in removing illiteracy, poverty, laziness and other social evils and bringing balance socio-economic, moral and spiritual development of all members of their society. The socio-economic backwardness of the Muslims is due to failure of their grassroot level leaders in providing right kind of guidance to their community because of their intellectual backwardness and selfishness and lack of their vision and mission.

The Muslims have hardly any propensity to save a portion of their income and form capital to meet their future needs. This is because of the fact that their level of income is much lower than what they require to meet their individual and family needs. Saving is possible only when the income is more than what is needed. If the income is just enough, even than a portion of the income can be saved for future use by cutting down the level of present consumption of less important goods and services. But the level of income and employment among the Muslims of Meghalaya is so low that the average Muslim can hardly think of saving a portion of their income. However, this scenario should not be allowed to deter them from making effort to develop their economic status. They should work hard with sincerity and devotion and try to avail all facilities offered by the government to raise their level of income and develop habit to save a portion of their income among themselves for meeting their future contingencies. There is no substitution of hard work. The Holy Qur'an says: "Lo! Allah changeth not the condition of a folk until they (first) change that which is in their hearts"[1]

While making saving to form capital for investment for furthering their income, the Muslim should remember that they should be judicious in both spending and saving. There is no place for niggardliness or prodigality in Islam. The Holy Qur'an says: "And let not thy hand be chained to thy neck nor open it with a complete opening, lest thou sit down rebuked, denuded"[2].

After the satisfaction of the legitimate requirement of the family and dependents, savings for meeting the needs of the future and posterity are allowed. But saving more than what is enough is prohibited in Islam. The Holy Qur'an says: "Woe unto every slandering traducer, who hath gathered wealth of this world and arranged it. He thinketh that his wealth will render him immortal."[3] The surplus amount is to be, instead of hoarding, spent or invested for the welfare of the poor and destitute of the community. The income generation efforts will continue to spend more and more for the cause of Allah. The Holy Qur'ãn has made this clear thus: "And strive with your wealth and your lives in the way of Allah"[4]. Wealth is not the end but a powerful means for achieving the end, that is, success in the world and in the Hereafter. The objective of the business enterprise in Islam is to earn wealth for only satisfying man's material requirements and pleasing Allah.

The problem of capital of the Meghalaya Muslims can be gradually overcome by taking up co-operative business enterprise on the basis of profit and loss sharing principle propounded by Islamic scholars in the light of Holy Qur'an and Hadith. Co-operation can be defined as the process of putting a group of people together, weather it is small or large, in the endeavour of achieving mutually agreed, legally permissible, well-defined common economic objective. It is in conformity with the Islamic concept and spirit of brotherhood, equality and unity. The Holy Qur'an instructs: "And co-operate with each other in good works of piety and God-fearing. Help not one another unto sin and transgression."[5]

The Muslims of every locality should strive collectively to ameliorate their plight. The community, which is divided, cannot flourish. Allah knows this best. In the Holy Qur'ãn, He, therefore, says: "And hold fast all of you to the rope of Allah and do not separate. And remember Allah's favour unto you how ye were enemies and He made friendship between your hearts so that ye became as brothers by His grace."[6] The Muslims should always choose a person from among themselves as their leader whose character and conduct is best of all of them to lead them in their effort of their material and spiritual well being. The Holy Qur'an says: "O mankind! Lo! We have created you male and female, and have made you nations and tribes that ye may know one another. Lo! The noblest of you in the sight of Allah, is the best in conduct. Lo! Allah is Knower, Aware."[7] The Muslims should strive in such a manner so that every one of them is able to be at ease and maintain their wives, children and dependents, pay Zakat, Fitrah and Sadaqah and perform Hajj at least once in his lifetime.

The relationship of the Muslims with other communities of the state should be peaceful and cordial. There should be no room left for misunderstanding, tension and conflict in their relationship with others, particularly with the major communities in the state. This will provide new scope for investment and development in their economic front.

The call of the hour for the Muslims is that every one of them should present himself or herself as the true model of Islam and strives with his or her wealth and life for the success in both the worlds. There is no alternative to this for achieving success for them. The Holy Qur'an says: "By the declining day, lo! Man is in state of loss, save those who believe and do good works, and exhorts one another to truth and exhorts one another to endurance."[8]

Let every one of us hope for success and strive in the way of Allah and pray in the language of Qur'an thus: "Our Lord! Give us good in this world and good in the Hereafter and protect us from the fire of Hell."[9] (Ameen)

ENDNOTES

1. The Holy Quran Surah XIII: Ayah 11
2. Ibid. Surah XVII: Ayah 29
3. Ibid. Surah CIV: Ayah 1 – 3
4. Ibid. Surah IX: Ayah 41
5. Ibid. Surah V: Ayah 2
6. Ibid. Surah III: Ayah 103
7. Ibid. Surah XLIX: Ayah 13
8. Ibid. Surah CIII: Ayah 1 –3
9. Ibid. Surah II: Ayah 201

APPENDIX A

IMPORTANT PERSONALITIES

Abdul Matlib Mazumdar (1890 -1990) – He was one of the prominent political leaders of Assam. He became cabinet minister for the first time in Gopinath Bordoloi ministry in 1946 and held the portfolio of Local-self government, Vetenary and agriculture. He was also a minister in the Bishnu Ram Medhi and Bimala Prasad Chaliha ministries. He was against the inclusion of the Surma Velley into Pakistan. He was known for his simplicity, piety, honesty and sincerity.

Aurangzeb (1618 – 1707) – Aurangzeb, the third son of Shah Jahan, ascended to the throne of Delhi in 1658 at the age of 39 years. By his diplomacy, military skill, courage and sheer determination, he had not only consolidated his position as a ruler but also established a vast empire in India. Aurangzeb was a truly religious, righteous and honest man. He respected all religion equally and allotted land liberally to his Hindu subjects for construction of their places of worship. He had profound knowledge of Arabic and Persian languages. Under his guidance the famous Muslim Law book, Fatwa-e-Alamgir, was composed. Being a pious man, he never indulged in luxury nor drank a drop of wine in his life. After ruling India for fifty years, he breathed his last at the age of 89 years on March 3, 1707. He was a powerful ruler and a wise politician.

Brington Buhui Lyngdoh (1922-2003)-Born in the Village of Laitlyngkot in Present East Khasi Hills district in February 1922, Lyngdoh did his school education in the Ramakrishna Mission School, Cherrapunji and passed his matriculation examination in 1944. He passed his intermadiate science examination from Guwahati Cotton College and did his B.A. and LLB from the Calcutta university. He started his career as a teacher.

Lyngdoh Shot to fame as a leader of the hill state movement. In 1962 he was elected to the Assam Legislative Assembly from Nongpoh constituency. In 1970 he became which was created within Assam in 1969 and inaugurated on April 2, 1970. Later, he had the opportunity to become chief minister of Meghalaya for four times. He became chief minister of the state for the first time in 1979 and held the office till may 7, 1981. He was chief minister of the state from March 10, 1998 to March 31, 2000 for the last time. He died on October 27, 2003 after a brief illness. He was well-known to all sections of the people for his honesty, sincerity and board social outlook. He was an astute Politician.

Captain Williamson A. Sangma (1919-2003)-He was vibrion Politician of Meghalaya. He was born on October 18, 1919 in a village near Siju in Present South Garo Hills district. He recieved his school education in Goalpara and college education in Dhaka and Serampore. He began his career as an army Officer in August-1942, the year of quite India Movement. He left the army in 1946 and then jooined Politics. In 1947 he became the President of the Garo National conference. In 1950 he founded Eastern India

Tribal Union alongwith other hill leaders and raised the demand for formation of a seperate hill state for the tribals of Assam.

Captain Sangma was elected to the post of Chief Executive Member (C.E.M.) of the Garo Hills Autonomous district council twice. In January 1958 he resigned from the post of C.E.M. and joined B.P. Chaliha cabinet as the minister of Tribal Affairs etc. In 1960 he resigned from the Caliha cabinet in protest against making Assamese official language of Assam and formed All-party Hill Leaders' conference to carry out the movement for creation of a seperate hill state.

In 1969 the Autonomous state of Meghalaya was created within Assam. On April 2, 1970 the Autonomous state was inaugurated and captain Sangma became the first chief minister of it. After Meghalaya was declared as full fledged state on January 21, 1972, he became chief minister of the state for two full terms. He also served as a governor of Mizoram for brief period. His eventfull life came to an end on October 25, 1990. He was loved and respected by all sections of the people.

Fakhruddin Ali Ahmed – He was veteran politician of Assam. He was first included in the Bordoloi ministry as cabinet minister in 1938. In 1952 he was elected as a member of Rajya Sabha. During the period from 1957 to 1965 he was cabinet minister of Assam and held the portfolios of Finance, Law, Community Development, Panchayat and Local-self Government. On January 29, 1966, he joined Union Council of Ministers as cabinet minister for Irrigation and power. He also served as union minister for Education, Industrial Development of Company Affairs and Food and Agriculture. On August 21, 1974, he was elected as the fifth President of Indian Republic as the Congress nominee and held the post till his death on February 11, 1977.

Giasuddin Auliya – He came to Assam to preach the message of Islam from Makkah in 14th century A.D. and stayed at Gaururachal hill of Hajo. He lived there in a cave for over two decades till 1350 – 1351. His tomb is located al-Gaururachal hill which is situated at about 750 feet above the ground just in front of the mosque which he had established for the congregational prayer of the new converts of Islam at a spot where he enshrined a lump of soil that he had brought from Makkah with him. It is said that the mosque was rebuilt by Muhammad sujauddin, the second son of emperor Shahjahan, when he was governor of Bengal and Hajo was under the direct rule of the Mughal. Giasuddin Auliya shot to fame as a preacher and saint. Many people in and around of Hajo came to the fold of Islam impressed by his teaching and became his disciples.

Gopinath Bordoloi (1891 – 1950) – After obtaining his B.A. and B.L. degrees from Calcutta University, Bordoloi started his political career. In 1938 he constituted the Congress coalition ministry in Assam but resigned on November 15,1939 in protest against involving India into the Second World War by the British at the direction of the Congress Working Committee. In 1946 he again formed the Congress ministry and remained the chief minister of Assam until his death in 1950. During his tenure of chief minister-ship thousands of Muslims were evicted from Assam. During the communal riots of 1948 – 1950, countless Muslim houses were burnt down and many of them killed and five to six lakhs lakh Muslims compelled to leave Assam for East Pakistan under duress.

Mahatma Gandhi (1869 – 1948) – He is one of the greatest Indian leaders of the 20th century. He was exponent of truth and non-violence and worked for communal harmony and abolition of untouchability. He successfully led the Indian people to achieve their freedom from the British yoke. He is called the father of the Indian nation. He was assassinated by godse in 1948. His famous work is *The Story of My experiment with Truth.*

Mir Jumlah – He was very brave and intelligent general of Mughal emperor Aurangzeb. In 1596, Laxmi Narayan, the king of Coch Bihar, declared himself as the vessel king of the Mughal empire. In 1657, Pran Narayan, the then Coch king, occupied Goalpara, Northern Kamrup and Hajo from the local Mughal administration and declared himself independent. Ahom king Jayadhvaj Singha also occupied Guwahati, Pandu and Saraighat from the Mughals. At this juncture, Mughal emperor Aurangzeb appointed Mir Jumlah as the governor of Bengal and Orissa and assigned him the responsibility to recover the lost territory from the Koches and the Ahoms. On November 1, 1661, Mir Jumlah launched his expedition to Assam. On December 19, 1661, he recovered Coch Bihar from Pran Narayan. Then on January 4, 1662, he proceeded to the Ahom kingdom and by March 17, 1662, conquered the entire Ahom kingdom including its capital, Garhgaon. He then established a mint at Garhgaon and stroke coin there in the name of emperor Aurangzeb. On January 23, 1663 he concluded a treaty with Jayadhvaj Singha. As per the treaty, the territory west of the Barnadi River on the north bank of the Brahmaputra to the Kalang on the south went under the Mughal rule. After the conclusion of the treaty, while Mir Jumlah was returning to Dacca, he fell sick and died on March 30, 1663 before reaching Dacca.

Moidul Islam Bora (1899 – 1944) – He is the first Assamese to obtain doctorate degree. He rendered Mirza Nathan's Baharistan-e-Gaibi into English from Persian into two volumes in 1936. Mirza Nathan was an important army officer of Mughal Kamrup during the period from 1612 to 1625.

Moulana Abul Kalam Azad (1888 – 1958) – He was one of the front ranking leaders in the freedom movement of India. He was a leader of great talent and unsurpassed sincerity and honesty. He was elected president of the All India Khilafat Committee. In 1923 he was elected as the president of the Indian National Congress for the first time. In 1940 he was again elected to the post and held the position continuously till 1945. After independence of India, Moulana Azad became the first education minister of India and held the portfolio until his death on February 22, 1958. He edited and published two Urdu dailies, namely, Al-Hilal (1912 – 1914) and Al-Balagh (1915 – 1916). Among his published works, Tarjuman-al-Qur'an and India wins freedom are famous. He visited Shillong in 1938 to help Gopinath Bordoloi in forming government after the resignation of the Saadullah ministry. But at that time Bordoloi did not have the support of the majority members of the Assam Legislative Assembly and horse-trading was in full swing. Since Moulana was a man of excellent integrity and morality, he left the matter of forming the government in the state in the hands of the local leaders and went back from Shillong.

Moulana Abdul Hamid Khan Bhasani – He was a prominent freedom fighter and peasant leader of Assam. He actively participated in Khilafat and Non-cooperation movements. Obtaining education in a madrasah in Rangpur, he started his career as a teacher. Later on, he joined politics and shot to fame as peasant leader. He migrated to Dhubri and settled down in a river basin which was, afterwards, became known as the Bhasanirchar. He was well known for his piety, honesty and sincerity in Assam. People respected him as pir and sought his guidance even in religious matters. After independence of India, he migrated to East Pakistan.

Moulana Muhammad Tayyabullah (1894 – 1966) – He was the president of Assam Pradesh Congress Committee during 1940 – 1948 and played leading role in Assam in the freedom movement of India during the period from 1921 to 1947. The British government imprisoned and detained him for eight and half years. In 1947 he was elected to Assam Assembly and became minister of Excise, Information & Public Relations and Prison in the Bordoloi cabinet and remained so till 1950. He was elected to Rajya Sabha for two terms during 1956 – 1964. He was not only a political leader and a freedom fighter but also a reputed writer, philosopher and scholar of Assam. He authored a good number of books. Some of them are *Islam and Non-cooperation, Between the symbol and the Idle at last* and *Karagaror Chhiti.* The *Karagaror Chhit* is collection of letters written by him from prison to his daughter. In these letters his political thought and love for Assam as well as India have found vivid expression.

Muhammad Tayyabullah was born in Guwahati in1894 and passed his matriculation in1909. He did his B.Sc. from the Presidency College, Calcutta and M.Sc. in Mathematics from Calcutta University. He started his career as a teacher of Jamia Millia in 1922, but resigned from the post in 1924 and returned to Guwahati. Then he obtained Law degree and started his legal profession and joined the freedom movement. He passed away on October 30, 1966. He was a man of great intellect and piety.

Prophet Muhammad (570 – 633) – He is the last Prophet of Islam. Born in a respectable family of Makkah, he became wellknown as As-Sadiq and Al-Amin (Trustworthy) for his excellent integrity, honesty and sincerity of his personality from his childhood. He married Khadijah, a rich widow, at the age of 25 years, and attained Prophet-hood at the age of 40 years. He received the first revelation in the cave of the Hira. Enduring all humiliations, abuses and persecutions heaved upon him, he preached the message of Islam undauntedly and successfully brought all the Arabs into the fold of Islam and thus established the vast empire of Islam. He was at a time a leader of the Ummah, head of the state and religion, a teacher, a philosopher, an educationist, a statesman, a general, a reformer, a lawgiver, a humanist, a judge and a social activist but led a simple and humble life. He was chosen by Almighty Allah and blessed with all noble qualities that no man before and after him had or will have in future. He is undoubtedly the greatest man who ever born on this earth. He returned to immortal Allah at the age of 63 years in 633 A.D.

Saleh Md. Akbar Hydari – He was the governor of Assam during the period from May 4, 1947 to December 28, 1948. He played the vital role in integrating the Naga Hills and the Khasi-Jaintia Hills into the Union of India. He was an honest, upright and hard working man and enjoyed full confidence and respect of the tribal people because of his august personality.

Sheikh Muhammad Amjad Ali (1868 – 1920) – Born in Sylhet in 1868, Amjad Ali did his school education in Shillong and passed his matriculation examination in 1887. While studying in school, he learnt the Khasi language and composed a large number of poems in Khasi. He published his first poetical work, 'Ka Myntoi' (The Profit) from Calcutta in 1888 and shot to fame as the first poet in the Khasi language. He obtained his Law degree from Calcutta in 1892 and returned to Shillong. Starting his career as a clerk, Amjad Ali retired as Assistant Inspector General of Prison, Assam in 1920. In 1923 he was elected to the Assam Legislative Council. He was also legal adviser of the Syiem (king) of Myllyiem and elected Commissioner of Shillong Municipal Board. He was famous as poet, lawyar and social activist. He died at the age of 78 years at his residence at Laban in Shillong on January14, 1936. He was a friend, philosopher and guide of the tribal people.

Syed Muhammad Saadullah (1885 – 1955) - Born on May 21, 1885 in Guwahati, S. M. Saadullah took his early education in Guwahati and passed his entrance examination from Sonaram High School, Guwahati. Then he went to Calcutta for further study and obtained his M. Sc. degree in Chemistry from Calcutta University. He also obtained Law degree from the Earl Law College, Guwahati. His forefathers came to Assam from Makkah in1633. Saadullah began his career as a lecturer of Cotton College, Guwahati. But within a short time he left the job and joined politics. He became member of the first Assam Legislative Council in 1913 and held the position till 1920. In 1924 he became minister of Education and Agriculture. In 1930 he again became minister of Finance and Law and Order. Later on, he practiced law for sometime in Calcutta High Court. On April 1, 1937, he became the first premier of Assam and remained so till February 11, 1946 with a break of about eighteen months. He was the opposition leader in the Assam Legislative Assembly during the period from 1946 to 1950. He breathed his last on January 8, 1955. He was well known for his experience, honesty, sincerity and broad social outlook.

Shah Jalal – He is a 14th century Muslim saint of Yemen. He came to Sylhet with Sikandar Gazi who conquered Sylhet in 1384. He became very popular in Sylhet as a saint and had 360 disciples who spread to different places and preached the massage of Islam among the local tribes. As a result, a large number of people came to the fold of Islam. It is said that his uncle sent him to India with a lump of soil and asked him to settle in a land whose soil is similar to that of the soil given by him. Shah Jalal found the soil of Sylhet similar with the soil given by his uncle and settled down there.

Shah Kamal – He was a Muslim saint. It is said that he came from Bengal to Garo Hills. The date of his coming to Garo hills could not be ascertained due to non-availabity of records. However, Shah Kamal, the son of sayed Jamel Khan, became popular in the western foothills of Garo hills for helping the people in distress. He was respected by all sections of people. His tomb is situated at a distance of four kilometres from Mahendraganj on the north.

Shah Milan – Shah Milan came to Assam in1635 from Baghdad and acquired a very prominent place in Assamese society. He preached Islam and introduced the Practice of calling Azan before offering prayer in Assam and therefore, became known as Azan pir. He learnt Assamese and composed Zikr containing teachings of Islam in simple and unambiguous language and made them familiar in Assamese society. Some officials of the then Ahom King hatched a conspiracy against him and charged him as a spy of the Mughals. Following this allegation, his eyes were pulled out but later on, the charge leveled against him proved false. The Ahom king regretted his action and honoured him with title, 'Debang.' After his death, Azan Pir was buried at Suraguri Chapori in Sibsagar. The Muslims and the Hindus alike respect his tomb.

APPENDIX B

RECOGNIZANCE OF OOPHAR RAJAH OF BHAWUL POONJEE, 1832

Seal of Oophar Rajah

To

The Agent of the Governor-General

I, Oophar Rajah, resident of Bhawul Poonjee, have this day, of my own free will and accord, and without any compulsion, executed this Recognizance before Captain Townshend, at Cherra Poonjee, as detailed in the following paragraphs, and I will be responsible for the violation of any of the terms thereof, and will obey the orders of the gentlemen.

1. That if the Cossiahs should kill, or in any way harm or injure any of the honorable Company's people within the boundaries of the Ooahn Churra of Hatee Khodda on the west, and the Dhoolai Nuddee on the west bank of the Dongdongiah on the east, I will immediately produce the guilty persons and make reparation for the losses sustained.

2. That, I will not give any shelter, assistance or provisions to enemies of the Honourable Company, and whenever I may receive any news regarding them, I will send information thereof to the Government's people through the Dooahradars.

3. That, I will not allow any of the Honourable Company's

enemies to come to my Ahrung of Seemai when it is reopened.

4. That whenever I may be called for by the Gentlemen, I will attend immediately on receipt of the written order to do so, and if I act contrary to the stipulations made in the above paragraphs, I will submit to any orders the Gentlemen may choose to pass; to which end I have executed this Recognizance.

Dated the 11th December, 1932, corresponding with 27th Ahgan, 1239 B.S.

Witnessed by:

Goopeeram, resident at present at Chattarkonah

Askur Mahmed, resident of Pergunnah Mahram, Mouzah Nolegong

Rohoomot Dooahradar, resident of Ghasegong

Ramjan Dooahradar, resident of Pergunnah Mahram, Mouzah Kandeegon

Robaie Dooahradar, resident of Chorogong

Source: Kumar B.B., The trends of British annexation of North-East India, 1994, Omsons Publications, New Delhi – 110027

APPENDIX C

AGREEMENT WITH THE WAHADADARS OF CHEYLA POONJEE, 1829

(Sd.) Mishnee Wahadadar
" Bursing Wahadadar
" Soomon and Ooksan Wahadadars
Residents of Cheyla Poonjee

To

The Honourable Company

The written Agreement of Mishnee, Bursing, Soomon and Ooksan, Wahadadars of Cheyla Poonjee, and other villages, twelve in number; Whereas a disturbance or battle took place in the Hills, and we did not join with the Government or make our appearance, in consequence of which troops were sent to our villages; we now come forward and give this agreement to abide by the following stipulations:

1. That, having committed these faults, we agree to pay installments to Government, amongst our twelve villages, a fine of Rupees 4,000 for the payment of which we four persons are responsible.
2. That, from the limestone situated on the banks of the Bogah river in our territory, we agree to allow the Government always to remove gratis, as much as they require, in any locality selected by their officers, but it is not to be taken from any other place.

3. That should any persons concerned in any act in Zillah Sylhet or other places, come and take shelter with us, we will immediately deliver them up on their being called for by the Zillah courts.

4. That, we promise not to dispute or make war with the Honourable Company, or with any of the Rajahs who are in confederacy with the Government.

5. That, if any quarrels should arise between us, and the Rajahs alluded to, the Government is to investigate and settle them, and to this effect we have executed this Agreement.

Dated the 3rd September 1829, corresponding with the 19th of Bhadro, 1236 B.S.

Petition of the Wahadadars of Cheyla Poonjee to the Political Agent of the Coossiah Hills in 1851, soliciting his assistance in causing the attendance, at their Durbars, of persons resisting their authority and offering to abide by his decision in appeals preferred to him against their orders, or in complaints made to him against their acts.

(Sd.) Mishnee Wahadadar
" Bursing "
" Larsing and Sonarai Wahadadar
" Ookhang and Beekai "
Residents of Cheyla Poonjee

Source: (Kumar B.B., The trends of British Annexation of North-East India, 1994, Omsons Publications, New Delhi – 110027)

APPENDIX D

SOME SELECTED POEMS FROM SHEIKH MUHAMMAD AMJAD ALI'S "KA MYNTOI", 1888

IENG 'RIW KHASI

To ieng, to ieng, ko 'Riw Khasi!
To ieng na la jingshong badum;
Da ka jinghok panpoh lade,
Rah u ding duh rah u sum,
To ieng, to ieng, ko 'Riw Khasi;
To dih ka um jingstad,
Ia ka Niam Pynbud ryngkat;
Mih ha thyma-ka jing pyrkhat.
Jimphong-is'nei to phong maphi
Panspong da jing shisha
To kup, to kup, jain-kup-sybun
To rah wait-jing-bha
To bat skhem ia u 'nam-minot
Ia ka ryntih- jing-mlin,
To ieng, to ieng, ko lok baroh!
Ioh phin shitom bad shah sin.

***

U TAI BAD U BADUK

Shi wat ki briw ki la kylli,
Ia u Sim Hatim Tai,
"Ba uei u don ba khraw naphi
Hangne ha ka pyrthei?"
La ong ma u ia ki hangta-
"U don uta uwei,
Ia ba la shem hamar hangta
Ha ba nga la iaid kai".
"Uta u briw u ba duk eh
Sha khlaw u la nang trei" :
La ong ia u "ko duk bapli,
To leit ha u Sim Tai".
"Phi'n ioh jingbam jingsa baroh
Katba phi mon phi kuah,
To leit, to khie, tymmem bapli,
Ba phi'n ioh suk shisha".
"La ong ia nga", "Balei ko pa!
Phi ong kumne ia nga,
Ba'n bam na u khyndiat ruh
Nga'm sngowbha."
"katba nga don la kti la kyjat
Katba nga nangtrei

Nga lehrain sngow ba poh shibun
Ba'n pan ba'n bam na'wei."

***

SYNSHAR 'RIW KHASI

Synshar, synshar, ko 'Riw Khas!
To synshar hi iaphi,
U Blei u'n rap baroh ia phi
Ba'n synshar maphi hi.
Balei phi'n leitlong braw
Ha ki nong-ong baroh,
U'n rap U'n rap U Blei ba khraw
Ha ba phi ia U iaroh
Phi'n ioh jingsuk shisha te phi
Khlem artatien artat,
Ha ba ia soh maphi hi
Ha ba phi leh da pyrkhat
Phi'nleit kylla mraw balei?
Ha ki jinglong nongwei
Khlem pyekhat ki jing hikai
Jong I Thawlang, Iawbei,
Synshar, synshar ko 'riw Khasi,

Synshar ia la jingmut;
Wat leh shukor, wat leh bishni,
Long ba shlur, wat long khawput,
Wad ka niam, wad ka jingstad,
Wad ka jingsuk Khasi:
Ia ka jingmut skhem to bat,
Bad pynshai ia la ka ri,
Synshar, synshar ko 'Riw Khasi!
Synshar ia la ki kur,
Ia ktin na ing wat ai baq'n mih,
Ioh u ksuid u'n sa tur,
Ia bam ia dih ia suk, ia neh,
Baroh shi kur shi lok.
Khlem ia dat khlem ia beh,
Hinrei da shong kum ki riw hok.
Synshar, synshar ko 'riw Khasi!
Synshar ia la jinglong,
Wat leit sha bar neh ha jilli,
Wat leh b'ymman, wat leh sarong

***

U LOBLI

La don uwei u nong-ia-pom
Hangta ha'wei ka por,
Ba la dykohna jing-ia –pom
Ba'n iaid ruh u'm don bor,
La don rungkat jong u hangta,
Tang u Lobli baieit,
U ba kumba hyniew snem ka'rta
U khynnah ba met rit.
Kumba kine shi wat mynmiet
Ha la ing ia ioh thiah,
Ba'n shim ia'ni khynnah baieit
Jing-jia-kyndit ia jia.
Ka pluh ka ing u nong-ia-pom,
Ba'n pynlip ym don briw,
Ia la ipa, na jing shitom
Ba'n leit, u la kyrsiw.
U'm ioh ktin na'ba nang thiah
(Namar b'ym don shuh)
Khlem kita u bein kynriah;
U shong u sah hajuh.
Ba'n bah, ba'n rah ia la ipa

U'm don bor satia,
Namar kata hajan jing thiah
U sah khlem kynriah.
Pat sah shi wat u kyrsiw
Ia la ipa ba'n khie;
Ka ding ka bur ha neng ka kiw
Hangta ruh u'm ioh hi.
Ka met ki jain ki la sydang
Ba'n ing, hangta jong u.
Pat sa shi wat u la ka'ng
U'm ioh kumta ruh.
Hajan ia la ipa u shong
Haduh b'nda u iap,
Baroh kawei ka ing ha jerong
Ka hap ka sop ka tap.

***

TOPU

Hangne hi ha La-ban
Don kawei ka briw.
Ba khlem khun khlem ksiw,
Ba la kydor ba la khun

Na u khnam ha ryntih.
Ha ka por jingshitom
Ha kane ka pyrthei
Ba'n iarap ia ka
Ym don mano mano
Lait na wei u ksew.
Ka jing ngeit u Topu,
Ia la ka trai kynrad.
La palat ia kita,
Jong ki khun bynriw ruh,
Ha ba ka leit shano shano,
U ju bud ia ka hi,
Bad ha ba ka ong ba'n wan noh
Sha la ing. U kylla din, bad
Wan khlem ar kyntin.
Ynda la poi ka por set,
Ia ki siar u ju wad;
Ynda la shem, ia ki u set
Da leh sumar; A! u mrad.
Ynda la set ia ki kumta
Da la ki kti ia ka jingkhang
Da sumar ba nym phet kita,

Mian mian ia ka u khang.
A! u mrad me long ba kyrpang.
'Da leh kumta sa ma u pat;
La shong ha khymat ka jingkhang
Kum u shakri u ba ngeit
Ynda ladep ki kam
Nang ap shuh ki jingphah
Na la u trai kynrad,
Ba la khreh ia lade
Ba'n leit kyllen ma u.
Kat by'm pat poi ka tymmen
Katta u'num ai ba'n wan
Ka mrad, Ka mreng, briw lada
Iano iano hajan ing ruh
Kum u shakri u ba ngeit Blei,
U by'm ju ai ba'n sniw
Ka hima jinghok jong U Trai
Ha khymat jong u khydiat ruh.
Ha ba u'n ih ia ki mrad
Lane ki sim, la ia puh
Lane ia dait : u'n pynkhlad
Ha kata hi khlem da ting.

Kum u rangbah na ki paitbah
U ba don bor bad ba hok,
Ba kuah jingsuk ha ka pyrthei
Ba 'nym ia shun para lok.

***

APPENDIX E

GENERAL SEATS OF MEGHALAYA LEGISLATIVE ASSEMBLY AND THE NUMBER OF ELECTORATES AS IN FEBRUARY 2003

General MLA seats	District	Number of Electorates
18 Pynthorumkhrah	East Khasi Hills	28,189
21 Mawprem	"	20,286
22 Laban	"	15,178
48 Phulbari	West Garo Hills	23,281
60 Mahendraganj	"	17,773

Total electors in Meghalaya as on February 2003 – 12,79,740

Source: The Meghalaya Guardian, February 4, 2003

NOTES

1. Total number of Meghalaya Legislative Assembly seats is 60. Out of this, 55 seats are reserved for the tribal communities of the state.
2. Two Muslim candidates of general category have chance to win election only in two Legislative Assembly constituencies – Phulbari and Mahendraganj – of the state.
3. Only One Muslim tribal candidate has a chance to win election from only Rajabala reserved Legislative Assembly Constituency provided the Muslims caste their vote en masse to their candidate. The total electors of this reserved constituency is 22,059 as in February 2003.

electors of this reserved constituency is 22,059 as in February 2003.

APPENDIX F

MUSLIM G.OVERNORS AND MINISTERS OF MEGHALAYA

I. Muslim governors of undivided Assam

1. Saleh Muhammad Akbar Hydari (May 4, 1947 – December 28, 1948)
2. Saiyid Fazl Ali (1957 – 1959)

II. Muslim governors of Meghalaya

1. A. A. Rahim (1988 –1989 & 1991)

III. Muslim ministers of Meghalaya

1. Abu Taher Mondal, Minister of State, (1998 -)
2. Abdus Saleh, Minister of State, (2001 - 2003)
3. Sayeedullah Nongrum, Cabinet Minister, (2003 -)
4. Manirul Islam Sarkar, Cabinet Minister, (2003 -)

APPENDIX G

MUSLIM POPULATION OF NORTH-EAST INDIA (AS PER 1991 CENSUS)

State	Total population	Muslims	Percentage of Muslims of the total population
Arunachal Pradesh	8, 64, 558	11, 922	1.38
Assam	2, 24, 14322	63, 73, 204	28.43
Manipur	18, 37, 149	1, 33, 535	7.27
Meghalaya	17, 74, 778	61, 462	3.46
Mizoram	6, 89, 756	7.301	0.66
Nagaland	12, 09, 546	20,683	1.71
Tripura	27, 57, 205	1, 96,495	7.13
Total of North -East India	**3, 15, 47,314**	**68, 01, 832**	**21.56**
Sikkim	4, 06, 457	3,861	0.95

APPENDIX H

WORDS OF ISLAMIC ORIGIN FOUND IN KHASI-JAINTIA AND GARO LANGUAGES OF MEGHALAYA

Words of Islamic origin	*Khasi-Jaintia*	*Garo*
Achar (Pickle)	Ashar	Achal
Atta (Floor)	Ata	Ata
Baba (Father)	—	Baba
Bakshish (Reward)	Boksis	Boksis
Chitthi (Letter)	Shithi	Chiti
Chalak (Clever)	Shalak	Chalak
Chalan (Export)	Shalan	Chalan
Dalil (Document)	Dolir	Dolil
Daroga (Police Inspector)	Dorka	Daroga
Dakhal (Possession)	Dakhar	Dokol
Darbar (Council/ Court)	Durbar	Dorbal
Dorji (Tailor)	Dorji	Dorji
Dastur (Custom)	Dustur	—
Dukan (Shop)	Dukan	Dokan
Dushman (Enemy)	Dusmon	—
Elaka (Area / Locality)	Elaka	Eleka
Fakir (Denouncer of the world)	Phukir	—
Gajor (Carrot)	Kajor	Gajor
Gulab (Rose)	Kulap	Gulap
Guli (Cartridge)	Kuli	Guli
Hazar (Thousand)	—	Hazal
Hazir (Present)	Hajir	Hajir
Hakim (Magistrate)	Hakim	Hakim

Haqq (Righteousness)	Hok	—
Hukum (Order)	Hukum	Hukum
Izzat (Honour)	Ijot	—
Jadoo (Charm)	Jadu	Jadu
Jarib (Survey)	Jurip	Jarip
Jelibee (A kind of sweet dish)	Jalabi	Julabi
Juta (Shoe)	Juti	Juta
Kachhari (Court)	Kachari	Kachari
Kamai (Income)	Kamai	Kamai
Khazana (Taxt)	Khajna	Kajina
Khajur (Date)	Khajur	Kejur
Kitab (Book)	Kitab	Kitab
Maf (Pardon)	Map	—
Mamla (Case)	Mamla	Mamla
Mulk (Country)	Muluk	—
Noqad (Cash)	Nokot	Nogot
Nasib (Fate)	Nusib	—
Nilam (Auction)	Lilam	—
Niyam (Rule)	Niam (Religion)	Niam
Phatak (Prison)	Phatok	Patok
Phansi (Execution by hanging by neck)	Phasi	Pasi
Piyaz (Onion)	Piat	—
Pulao (Rice cooked with ghee)	Pulaw	Pulao
Qatal (Murder)	Qotal	—
Qaidi (Prisoner)	Koidi	Koidi
Qynchi (Sissor)	Kynshi	Kenchi
Rakam (Kind)	Rukom (Custom)	—
Rumal (Handerkarship)	Rumal	Rumal
Roti (Bread)	Ruti	Ruti

Ray (Decree)	Rai	Rai
Sanduk (Box)	Synduk	Sunduk
Sarak (Road)	Surok	Sorok
Sabun (Soap)	Sabon	Sabon
Shaitan (Satan)	Soitan	Satan
Sud (Interest)	Sut	—
Tamasha (A show)	Tamasa	amasa
Thag (Cheat)	Thok	Togia
Zamin (Surety)	Jamin	Jamin

GLOSSARY

EXPLANATION OF SOME TERMS

Allah: Almighty God

Akher ka sngi: The Day of Judgement

Akhirat: The world Hereafter

Assalamu Alaikum: May peace be upon you

Azan: Call for prayer

Aulyia: Muslim Saint

Bismillahir Rahmanir Rahim: In the name of Allah, the Benificent, the Merciful

Cabliwala: Money-lender from Afghanistan

Chowdhury: Head of several sikdarship

Dirham: A silver coin

Duardar: Agent of Khasi King

Durbar: Council / court / meeting

Eidgah: A place where the Muslims offer their Eid prayer

Eid-ul-Fitr: Name of the Muslim festival. It is observed on the first day of Sawwal after the month long fasting in Ramadan

Eid-uz- Azha: A Muslim festival. It is observed on the tenth of Zil-hajja

Fitrah: Charity given before Eid-ul Fitr Prayer

Fouzdar: Military Officer

Hadith: Saying of the Holy Prophet, (peace be upon him)

Hajj: Pilgrimage to Makkah

Hakim: Judge or Makkah

Imam: One who leads congregational prayers

Islam: It means peace, purity and surrender of man's will to the will of Almighty Allah. It is derived from the word, Salam, which means peace.

Jama'at: Congregation

Jhum: Shifting cultivation

Jihad: Striving to the cause of Allah for the good of the Individual and the community

Kala-Azar: Black fever

Ka niam jong ki Khasi: Religion of the Khasis

Khutba: Sermon

Laskar: Head of the village court

Madrasah: Higher Institution of Muslim education

Mahal: A revenue division of the Mughal administration

Maktab: Primary institution of Muslim education

Matabar: Title of a headman of a village

Mehr: An alimony given by the husband to the wife. It is fixed at the time of marriage. The minimum Mehr is ten Dirhams or equal to the value of about thirty-two Grams of silver. There is no maximum limit to it.

Momin: A believer

Mouzadar: Head of a Mouza

Muezzin: A caller of Azan

Mukhtar: A clerk

Muslim: One who surrenders his will to the will of Allah

Niam: Name of Khasi religion

Parganah: A revenue division of administration

Qari: An expert in reciting the Holy Qur'an

Qazi: Muslim judge

Qur'an: The Holy Book of the Muslims

Qurbani: Sacrfice

Ramdan: The ninth month of the Arabic calandar: the month of fasting.

Sadaqah: Charity

Salat: Muslim prayer

Sicca Tanka: A kind of coin used as the medium of exchange in Mughal India

Sarkar: An administrative division of Mughal India

Shawwal: The tenth month of the Hijri era
Shulong: Name of a Khasi god
Sikdar: In-charge of collection of revenue of a village
Sirdar: Headman of a village
Syiem: Chief of a Khasi State
Thanedar: In-charge of police station
U Blei: Name of Khasi god
Wakf: Legacy
Zakat: The system in Islam to help poor and needy.
Zamindar: An estate-holder
Zikr: Remembrance of Allah
Zimmadar: An organizer

SELECT BIBLIOGRAPHY

Ahmad Mohammad Muhiuddin, Asomloi Musolmanor Agamon Aaru Sankritic Sangmisron, 2000, Published by Begum A. Akhtar, Anandanagar, Panigaon, Nagaon, Assam.

Akbar M., Enterpreneurship and Indian Muslims, 1990, Nanak publication Pvt. Ltd., New Delhi- 110002.

Allen B.C., Gait E.A., Howword H. F. & Allen C. G. H., Gazetteer of Bengal and North- East India, 2001, Mittal Publications, A-110, Mohan Garden, New Delhi - 110059.

Bareh Hamlet, Progress of Education in Meghalaya, 1996, Cosmo publications for Genesis Publishing Pvt. Ltd. 24- B, Ansari Road, Daryaganj, New Delhi- 110002.

Bhattacharjee Arun, Assam in Indian independence, 1993, published by K.M. Rai Mittal for Mittal Publications, A -110, Mohan Garden, New Delhi- 110059.

——— Census of India, 1971, Series- 13, Meghalaya.

Das A.K., Assam's Agony, 1982, Lancers Publications, New Delhi- 110048.

Datta P.N., Relations of the Khasis and Jaintias with their southern neighbours till the British intervention, Paper presented in the First Session of North - East India History Association, Shillong, 1980.

Dev B. J. & Lahiri D. K., Assam Muslims Politics & Cohesion, 1985, Published by K. M. Mittal, Mittal Publications, B-2 / 14-B, Lawrence Road, Delhi-110035.

——— District Level Statistics, 2002, Government of Meghalaya,

Directorate of Economics and Statistics, Meghalaya, Shillong.

Dutta Sushil Chandra, The North – East and Mughals (1661-1714), 1984, D.K. Publications, 29 / 9, Nangia Park, Shakti Nagar, Delhi – 110007.

Gait Edward, A History of Assam, 1984, LBS Publications, Guwahati, Assam.

Kar M, Muslims in Assam Politics, 1997, Vikash Publishing HousePvt. Ltd., 576 Masjid Road, Jangpura, New Delhi – 110014.

Kar P.C. Glimpses of the Garos, 1982, Garo Hills Books Emporium, Tura, West Garo Hills.

Luniya B.N., Evolution of Indian culture, 1990, Lakshma Narain, Agarwal Educational publications, Agra – 3.

Mackenzie A., A History of relations of the government with the hill tribes of North-East frontier of Bengal, 1884.

Mathur P.R.G., The Khasi of Meghalaya, 1979, Cosmo Publications, New Delhi.

Mazumdar Abdul Matlib: Birth Centenary Tributes (1890 – 1990), Edited by Anwaruddin Chowdhury.

———— Meghalaya District Gazetteer: Jaintia Hills, 1996, Edited by I. M. Simon, Directorate of Arts and Culture, Government of Meghalaya , Shillong.

———— Meghalaya District Gazetteer: Garo Hills, 1996, edited by I. M. Simon, Government of Meghalaya, Arts and Culture Department, Meghalaya, Shillong.

—— Muslim Situation in India, 1989, edited by Iqbal A, Ansari, Sterling Publisher Pvt. Ltd., New Delhi- 110016.

Nag Sajal, Roots of ethic Conflicts: Nationality Question in North-East India, 1990 Published by Ramesh Jain, Manohar Publications, 2/

6 Ansari road, Daryaganj, New delhi – 110002.

Picthall Marmaduke, The Meaning of the Glorious Qura'n, 1983, Taj Company, 3151, Turkman Gate, Delhi-110006

—— Pocket Statistical Hand Book 2000,Government of Meghalaya, Directorate of Economics and Statistics, Shillong.

—— Radiance Views Weekly, 17–23 January 1999, Jamia Nagar New Delhi- 110025.

Rao V.V., Hazarika N., A century of government and politics in North-East India Vol. 1, Assam (1874 – 1980), 1983, S. Chand & Company Ltd., Ram Nagar, New Delhi - -110055.

Rao V.V., Pakem B. & Hazarika N., A century of government and politics in North-East India, Vol. II Meghalaya, (1874-1983), 1984, S. Chand & Company Ltd, New Delhi – 110055.

Ray B. Dutta, Khasi Hills and Brahma Samaj Movement, Paper presented in the First Session of North-East India History Association, 1980, Shillong.

——— Report on Census of Meghalaya state Government Employees as on 31st March 2000, Government of Meghalaya, Directorate of Economics and Statistics, Shillong.

Rustomji Nari, Imperilled Frontiers: India's North-Eastern Borderlands, 1983, Oxford University Press, New Delhi -110002.

Siddiqi Dr. Muhammad Najatullah, Economics enterprise in Islam, 1990, Markazi Makataba Islami, Delhi – 110006.

——— Souvenir, Khasi Students' Union, 20th Anniversary, Celebration (1978 – 1998), Edited by Paul Lyngdoh.

——— The Hindustan Times, North-East Live, Saturday, September 6, 2001.

——— The Milli Gazette, Vol. 2, No. 19, 1 – 15 October, 2001, D-

84, Abul Fazal Enclave-1, Jamia Nagar, New Delhi-110025.

—— The Muslim & Arab Perspectives, Vol, 4, Issue 7-12 February, 1999, Edited by Dr. Zafarul-Islam Khan, D-84, Abul Fazal Enclave-1, Jamia Nagar, New Delhi - 110025.

Warjri E., The Shellah Wahadadarship: The Roots of Polity Formation in the War Area of East Khasi Hills District, Proceedings of North-East Endia History Association, Seventh Session, Pasighat 1986, edited and published by J.B. Bhattacharjee on behalf of North-East India History Association, Department of History, North-Eastern Hill University, Shillong.

INDEX